The Commandments
in
Contemporary Culture

The Commandments in Contemporary Culture

KIERAN BEVILLE

Tercentenary Publication

2010

The Commandments in Contemporary Culture– Published by the Rev. Dr. Ashish Amos of the Indian Society for Promoting Christian Knowledge (ISPCK), Post Box 1585, 1654 Madarsa Road, Kashmere Gate, Delhi-110006.

© Author, 2010

ISBN : 978-81-8465-106-5

Laser typeset by

ISPCK, Post Box 1585, 1654, Madarsa Road, Kashmere Gate, Delhi-110006.
Tel: 23866322/23

e-mail: *ashish@ispck.org.in • ella@ispck.org.in*

website: *www.ispck.org.in*

Printed at Cambridge Press, Delhi-110006.

The Commandments[1]

1. "You shall have no other gods before Me."

2. "You shall not make for yourself a carved image — any likeness *of anything* that *is* in heaven above, or that *is* in the earth beneath, or that *is* in the water under the earth; you shall not bow down to them nor serve them. For I, the LORD your God, *am* a jealous God, visiting the iniquity of the fathers upon the children to the third and fourth *generations* of those who hate Me, but showing mercy to thousands, to those who love Me and keep My commandments."

3. "You shall not take the name of the LORD your God in vain, for the LORD will not hold *him* guiltless who takes His name in vain."

4. "Remember the Sabbath day, to keep it holy. Six days you shall labour and do all your work, but the seventh day *is* the Sabbath of the LORD your God. *In it* you shall do no work: you, nor your son, nor your daughter, nor your male servant, nor your female servant, nor your cattle, nor your stranger who *is* within your gates. For *in* six days the LORD made the heavens and the earth, the sea, and all that

---

[1] Exodus 20:3-17.

is in them, and rested the seventh day. Therefore the LORD blessed the Sabbath day and hallowed it."

5. "Honour your father and your mother, that your days may be long upon the land which the LORD your God is giving you."

6. "You shall not murder."

7. "You shall not commit adultery."

8. "You shall not steal."

9. "You shall not bear false witness against your neighbour."

10. "You shall not covet your neighbour's house; you shall not covet your neighbour's wife, nor his male servant, nor his female servant, nor his ox, nor his donkey, nor anything that *is* your neighbour's."

Contents

Preface .... *ix*

Introduction .... *xiii*

You shall have no other Gods before Me   1

You shall not make for yourself a carved image   10

You shall not take the name of the LORD
your God in vain   20

Remember the Sabbath day, to keep it holy   27

Honour your father and your mother   45

You shall not murder   62

You shall not commit adultery   86

You shall not steal   105

You shall not bear false witness   114

You shall not covet   123

Conclusion **131**

Preface

Once a pastor told me that he preached The Commandments after forty years in ministry and regretted that he had not done so earlier. This intrigued me and I began to study these verses in Exodus. I had not intentionally avoided preaching this passage of Scripture but I think in the back of my mind I felt I should preach grace rather than the law. So The Commandments did not immediately make it onto my list of ideas for preaching.

When I eventually did preach a series of sermons on the Commandments I was surprised by the way they reflected the glorious grace of God. In fact this series of sermons had more of an impact than anything I had ever preached before. Not only is it remembered more but it appears to have achieved more. For example, when I preached, "You shall not commit adultery", a woman who was visiting the church that Sunday morning began to weep uncontrollably during the sermon. Afterwards I learned that she had issues relating to this topic. She was a recent convert and she told me that she had never fully understood or appreciated God's grace until that moment. There were other instances of the power of God breaking through at this time which was an affirmation for me and a blessing for others.

I cannot say that if I preached it again the same would happen, nor can I guarantee that others who preach it will experience the same kind of visitation of God's power. But I would encourage every believer to consider what God has to say in *The Commandments*. If we are receptive and responsive to His Word there will be times of blessing. It is my desire that those who look into this portion of Scripture will catch a glimpse of the glory of God and see God's grace perfected in Christ. The law points to Jesus and serves to teach us of our need for grace. The law tells us that we are failures and it helps us to find faith in Christ, who fulfilled its requirements. The law tells us that we are sinners in need of salvation and sanctification. The law convinces us that Christ is our only hope.

> My hope is built on nothing less
> Than Jesus' blood and righteousness.
> I dare not trust the sweetest frame,
> But wholly trust in Jesus' Name.
>
> On Christ the solid rock I stand;
> All other ground is sinking sand
>
> When darkness seems to hide His face,
> I rest on His unchanging grace.
> In every high and stormy gale,
> My anchor holds within the veil.
>
> On Christ the solid rock I stand;
> All other ground is sinking sand
>
> His oath, His covenant, His blood,
> Support me in the whelming flood.
> When all around my soul gives way,
> He then is all my Hope and Stay.

On Christ the solid rock I stand;

All other ground is sinking sand

When He shall come with trumpet sound,

Oh may I then in Him be found.

Dressed in His righteousness alone,

Faultless to stand before the throne.

On Christ the solid rock I stand;

All other ground is sinking sand[1]

---

[1] Edward Mote, 1797-1874.

Introduction

According to The Bible the Ten Commandments (also known as 'The Decalogue') were given by God to Moses on Mount Sinai approximately 3,500 years ago. This was during the early years of Israel's history as God's chosen people. These commands constitute part of the law of God disclosed in the Pentateuch (the first five books of the Old Testament). Initially they related specifically to those in covenant relationship with the God of the Jews. However, they have subsequently come to be regarded as a central component in the Christian tradition and are foundational to the Western system of jurisprudence which has prevailed in civilised society for more than two thousand years.

These commands do not constitute the entire law of God. Both the Old Testament and the New Testament contain many other prohibitions, regulations, rules, expectations, guidelines and teaching concerning right and wrong attitudes and actions. Nevertheless they form the core of God's law.

The phrase, 'Ten Commandments', comes from Scripture itself: 'So he [Moses] was there with the LORD forty days and forty nights; he neither ate bread nor drank water. And He wrote on the tablets the words of the covenant, the Ten Commandments' (Exodus 34:28). Deuteronomy says: 'He declared to you His covenant which He commanded you to perform, the Ten Commandments; and He wrote them on two tablets of stone' (4:13).

The purpose of the law is to show the sinfulness of people in their moral distance from God. As such it demonstrates humanity's need for a mediator if they are ever to approach God. The law outlines how people should live; under the government and guidance of God. The Commandments are about right relations with God and right relations with society. This element of the law expresses God's holy will for the life and behaviour of mankind and serves as a guide to society in promoting a civic code of conduct. The law convicts sinners, produces repentance and drives people to Christ. The law directs Christians in holy living.

Christian Attitudes

There are different Christian attitudes today concerning the law of God. There are diverse opinions about its relevance, authority and efficacy. There are two broad categories of understanding with regard to the law of God.

Firstly, there is the antinomian position. This refers to the belief that Christians need not obey the moral law. Antinomianism stresses Christian freedom from the condemnation of the law but it underemphasises the need of believers to confess sins daily and to pursue sanctification earnestly. Ultimately this leads to moral laxity.

Secondly, there is the legalist and moralist position which stresses Christian responsibility and obedience to such an extent that it becomes more than evidence of faith. In this latter position obedience comes to be seen as something necessary to justifying faith; a constituent element that inevitably undermines Christian assurance and joy. The legalist and moralist perspective produces a self-centred and excessively introspective piety.

This is one of the great flaws of Dispensationalism. J. N. Darby in an effort to avoid moralism identified the law as the way of salvation in the Mosaic dispensation, whereas he identified the gospel of grace as the way of salvation in the New Testament dispensation. The actual effect of this has been to shift thinking in the direction of antinomianism, especially with regard to the distinction between Christ as Saviour and Christ as Lord. Thus the church today needs to understand afresh the biblically balanced teaching on law and gospel. Such an understanding is foundational to balanced Christian living.

Three Categories of Law

The lawgiver places His law in the context of grace. Man was created a responsible creature and as such he is accountable to his creator. It follows that there must be a standard by which his responsibility can be assessed. This standard is the Law of God and is fully set out in the Scriptures. There is some confusion and muddled thinking amongst some Christians concerning this subject of the law of God. Some teach that it pertained to Israel and is solely Jewish in character. Others teach that the law belongs to the old covenant, but now, under the new covenant, that law has passed away. The argument is that the believer is no longer under law but under grace because the law, having been fulfilled by Christ, now has no place in the life of a Christian. Consequently scant attention is given to this matter in the pulpit today. In order to come to a right understanding of this matter, it is essential to have a biblical knowledge of what constitutes the law of God.

The law, as given on Mount Sinai, falls into three categories; ceremonial, judicial and moral, and these distinctions are important.

The ceremonial law, with its many offerings and sacrifices, ended with the first advent of Christ. He was the fulfilment of all that was typified by those ordinances and therefore, of necessity, they have ceased.

The judicial law set out the manner in which Israel's society was to be governed and regulated. This also passed away in A. D. 70 when the Jewish nation was scattered and therefore ceased to exist.

The moral law (the Ten Commandments) is the abiding law of God for all time and did not pass with the coming of Christ. Usually reference to the law of God in the New Testament refers to the Ten Commandments and there is never a hint given that this has been repealed. These commands are the transcript of holiness or the divine standard which was written first upon the heart of Adam before it was inscribed on tables of stone at Sinai. This Law is binding upon all men for all time. It is the standard to which man is responsible and to which he will be held accountable. To be faithful to God and to uphold this law in contemporary culture appears legalistic to many both outside and inside the church. But it is a serious matter for any person to dismiss the law of God as irrelevant.

The Revelation of God

The Commandments are not a secular code of ethics compiled to create and maintain an ordered society. It is not a system that was devised in the minds of ancient people in order to govern and control behaviour. These rules were not concocted by conference or committee. They do not represent the distilled wisdom of ancient peoples. On the contrary they were disclosed by God to mankind and, as such, reflect the mind and heart of God rather than the collective insight of particular people. It is, therefore, a sacred thing.

It is clearly stated in the New Testament that, 'the law *is* holy, and the commandment holy and just and good' (Romans 7:12). The apostle Paul goes on to say, 'the law is spiritual' (Romans 7:14). It is said of the 'blessed man' to whom the psalmist refers in Psalm 1 that, 'his delight *is* in the law of the LORD'. The apostle Paul concurs when he says, 'I delight in the law of God' (Romans 7:22).

Some Christians appear to have the distorted view that the law was given in wrath and that God does not act in this manner now because it is a time of grace. This is not so; the law was given by God in love. Thus the words of Deuteronomy: 'And he said: "The LORD came from Sinai, and dawned on them from Seir; He shone forth from Mount Paran, and He came with ten thousands of saints; from His right hand *came* a fiery law for them. Yes, He loves the people…" ' (33:2-3). It was certainly a 'fiery' law insofar as it was pure. It could not be otherwise, for it was God's law, setting out His standards and requirements.

In love for His creatures the true standard of holiness has been made plain. The law was intended for man's blessing. It was instilled in Adam, the head of the human race, from the beginning. It is a fallacy to say that the law originated at Sinai. Concerning the gathering of the manna it is stated in Exodus: 'Now it happened *that some* of the people went out on the seventh day to gather, but they found none. And the LORD said to Moses, "How long do you refuse to keep My commandments and My laws?" ' (16:27-28). This was *prior* to the issuing of the Commandments at Sinai. The Ten Commandments pertaining to obedience and love for God, love of one's neighbour, Sabbath observance,[1] marriage and so on go back to and indeed are part of creation.

---

[1] This will be clarified later.

Permanent and Authoritative

The Mosaic Law incorporated the moral law. But the Ten Commandments were always clearly distinguished from the ceremonial and judicial laws of Israel, which were not of permanent duration. The very manner in which the Ten Commandments were given shows that this law was unique and supreme as it was actually written by the finger of God: 'when He had made an end of speaking with him on Mount Sinai, He gave Moses two tablets of the Testimony, tablets of stone, written with the finger of God' (Exodus 31:18). The fact that it was not written on parchment but on tablets of stone may symbolise its permanence but the fact that it was written by the finger of God certainly signifies its supreme authority, because of its authorship.

The uniqueness of The Decalogue is also seen in that it was only the Ten Commandments which were deposited in the Ark of the Covenant (Exodus 25:16-21). The ceremonial and civil regulations were not deposited there. When the Lord took up his abode in Israel's midst, it was from the mercy seat immediately above this written Law of God (Exodus 25:22).

So the Ten Commandments were incorporated into the Law of Moses. Yet that law preceded Moses and continues throughout all ages. To teach, as some do, that with the advent of Christ all law is forever done away is a travesty of the truth and a failure to appreciate the abiding nature of the law of God.

It is departure from this law (which is binding upon all men) that lies at the very heart of the world's troubles. All lawlessness, in whatever form, stems from a breach of God's commands. The believer is not freed from this divine standard. He is not under its *condemning* power but he is under its *commanding* power.

The Decalogue is profoundly important and deserves to be closely examined in its detail. The first seventeen verses of Exodus 20 represent one of the most important sections of *The Bible*. It is a clear publication of God's mind. The opening words are significant: 'And God spoke all these words'. The words of God deserve attention. When Almighty God speaks it is incumbent upon all to listen. It is a duty to listen with reverence because every word is an oracle from heaven. Thus these words are to be received, believed, remembered, observed and taught: "And these words which I command you today shall be in your heart. You shall teach them diligently to your children, and shall talk of them when you sit in your house, when you walk by the way, when you lie down, and when you rise up" (Deuteronomy 6:6-7).

Every generation of believers is held accountable to God for transmitting the law of God to the generation following. The Christian cannot impart God's grace to his children or to anyone else, but he can impart God's law and this is demanded. Concerning the commandments of the Lord, Scripture says, 'You shall teach them to your children' (Deuteronomy 11:19). It might be argued that fallen people cannot keep these commandments. This is true. Nevertheless we are to teach them and by God's grace in as much as is possible to keep them too. The Scriptures give the reason for this: 'Therefore by the deeds of the law no flesh will be justified in His sight, for by the law *is* the knowledge of sin' (Romans 3:20). This is why parents are to teach their children the law of God. This is why preachers are to preach that law. Only in this way are people made aware of sin and their standing before a holy God.

There are many things in the world today which are commonplace, which people do not realise are grievous in the sight of a holy God. It is commonly believed that the law of God has no relevance in today's society but the Christian should know better: 'Therefore the law was our tutor *to bring us* to Christ, that we might be justified by faith' (Galatians 3:24). A tutor is one who instructs and educates and this is exactly what the law does. When knowledge of sin is brought home to a person by such instruction, then they become aware of their need for a Saviour and may seek Christ. The crying need of this decadent age is the preaching of the law, the faithful proclamation of all these words which God spoke. But these words are not just a list of dos and don'ts.

A Profound Prologue

In examining them carefully it may be seen that there is a noteworthy preface. These introductory and preliminary remarks put the Commandments in context. This context is crucial in interpreting the law. This brief prologue reads, " I *am* the LORD your God, who brought you out of the land of Egypt, out of the house of bondage" (Exodus 20:2). For the sake of analysis it can be divided into three parts. First, "I am the Lord your God"; second, "Who brought you out of the land of Egypt" and third, "Out of the house of bondage". These three statements need to be examined.

Firstly, in the statement, "I am the Lord your God", the word for *Lord* here is *Jehovah*. This title sets forth the majesty of Israel's God. Jehovah, to this Old Testament people, was a name held in reverence above any other name. It signified to them the eternal nature and unchanging character of the Almighty God. This is emphasised in another Mosaic passage: "If you do not carefully observe all the words of this law that are written in this book, that you may fear this glorious and awesome name, THE LORD YOUR GOD" (Deuteronomy 28:58). The immutability of God is clearly declared in Malachi, "For I *am* the LORD, I do not change" (Malachi 3:6). In these references the word Jehovah is the word translated as

"LORD". So it is the eternal, unchanging Jehovah who enunciates His law and adds "YOUR GOD". There is a great deal implied by that little word *your*. It must have been wonderfully reassuring for them to know that the eternal, unchanging Jehovah was their God. The law was not given in anger. There was nothing unreasonable or legalistic in Jehovah emphasising a right code of conduct for a people to whom He was God, creator and redeemer.

Secondly, the statement, "who brought you out of the land of Egypt", is interesting. As this law is about to be announced, God reminds Israel of the deliverance which He effected for them. Consider the mighty signs and wonders of the plagues. Remember the covering of blood, from the Passover lamb, sprinkled on the doorposts, and consequent sparing of the first-born of Israel. Think about the dramatic parting of the Red Sea until all the children of Israel had passed over. Then, when the oppressor's armies were in hot pursuit, in the middle of the sea-bed, those walls of water gave way and all Egypt's army perished. God is turning their minds back to that pivotal time in their redemption and reminding them that the majestic Jehovah is the one who wrought all this for them.

Thirdly, the phrase, "out of the house of bondage" is not merely a repetition of the previous statement ("who brought you out of the land of Egypt"). There is a more profound thought conveyed here. Egypt, in biblical terms, speaks of the world of heathendom, idolatry and isolation from God. Israel's experience of Egypt was one of captivity and slavery. The "house of bondage" speaks of affliction and tyranny. God reminds Israel of that miserable exile and their slavery and humiliation. They had known the bitter experience of having to make bricks without the supply of materials. They had experienced cruel floggings by their harsh taskmasters. It was from such a terrible situation that God emancipated them.

This opening statement, "I am the LORD your God, who brought you out of the land of Egypt, out of the house of bondage", appears 125 times in Scripture. It was such a profoundly important event in the history of Israel that it was frequently repeated. There is a danger that we might come to see it as a boringly repetitive cliché or hackneyed phrase, so it is important to examine the significance of these words.

So it is with these introductory remarks that God began to issue these commands. God had dealt most graciously with these people. Thus it was entirely appropriate for God to present this law as a guiding system for living. There is no conflict here between law and grace. Some people are resentful of the commandments because it appears to impose constraints on liberty. It is often seen in negative terms as a list of prohibitions. People don't want to be restrained, especially in such an apparently authoritarian manner; "You shall not…"

The unchanging, sovereign, infallible God spoke 'all these words' for a reason. There is no denying that much of the Decalogue is expressed in negative terms but this is because of the shocking depravity of those to whom it is addressed. A prohibition presupposes a disposition to do that which is prohibited. In other words, if people were not inclined to worship other gods, then there would be no need for the first commandment. Similarly if there was no rebellious or disobedient spirit in a child, the fifth commandment, to honour parents, would be pointless. If no spirit of revenge or hatred ever possessed people it would be unnecessary to state, "You shall not murder". Adultery is forbidden because lust (which is essentially an adulterous, self-gratifying desire) is a reality. People are prone to lie and to bear false witness and so on. This is why the New Testament states, 'What purpose then *does* the law *serve?* It was added because of transgressions…' (Galatians 3:19).

A Different Perspective

God published His law in writing to all people for all time because of people's depravity. Many people recoil at the notion that they are depraved because they have been taught that they are evolving from a lower order of life and that they are on an inexorable ascent to a higher order. The reality of moral depravity evidenced and reported in the media simply contradicts that assumption. The truth is that people have a natural tendency to all manner of sin. Many people reject notions of right and wrong and utterly despise the word *sin* but that does not mean there is no such thing as right and wrong or that sin is merely an antiquated term.

It is true, in one sense, that the law is negative insofar as it instructs and restrains, but cannot implant positive virtue. The law of itself can never transform a sinful heart. Nevertheless it is a most vital part of Scripture. It is part of God's wonderful revelation and counsel.

Scripture establishes the abiding authority of the Ten Commandments as the moral Law of God. The New Testament speaks of the law in the following terms: 'By this we know that we love the children of God, when we love God and keep His commandments. For this is the love of God, that we keep His commandments. And His commandments are not burdensome' (1 John 5:2-3). This is quite a different perspective from those who understand the commandments as something which could inhibit their freedom and curtail their joy. But God does not deprive people of the opportunity to live a meaningful life. On the contrary Jesus said that He had come to impart abundant life (John 10:10). It is in right relationship with God that people reach their full potential. Life without a meaningful relationship with God can be burdensome. That is why Jesus extends the gracious invitation: "Come to Me, all *you* who labour and are heavy laden, and I will give you rest. Take My yoke upon you and learn from Me, for I am gentle and lowly in heart, and you will find rest for your souls. For My yoke *is* easy and My burden is light" (Matthew 11:28-30).

Understanding True Obedience

Isaiah 1 is a passage of Scripture that speaks of the wickedness of Judah. They had become a people who were evil and corrupt. They had forsaken the Lord and provoked Him to anger. Yet God had graciously spared a remnant of His people. Isaiah exhorted them to obedience and invited them to repent. In a very potent passage of Scripture God told His own people that even brute beasts are better at acknowledging their owners and masters than they were in recognising to whom they belonged and to whom they owed their obedience. They had continued to practice the external religious rites and rituals without sincerity.

Thus the Lord told them that He despised their sacrifices and that their religious observance was an abomination to Him and that their prayers were futile. The Lord graciously invited them to cleanse themselves and amend their behaviour. It is a very stern rebuke to a disobedient people and teaches us that God requires obedience. Here are selected verses from that chapter:

"To what purpose *is* the multitude of your sacrifices to Me?" Says the LORD. "I have had enough of burnt offerings of rams and the fat of fed cattle. I do not delight in the blood of bulls, Or of lambs or goats. "When you come to appear before Me, who has required this from your hand, to trample My courts? Bring no more futile sacrifices; Incense is an abomination to Me. The New Moons, the Sabbaths, and the calling of assemblies — I cannot endure iniquity and the sacred meeting. Your New Moons and your appointed feasts My soul hates; They are a trouble to Me, I am weary of bearing *them*. When you spread out your hands, I will hide My eyes from you; Even though you make many prayers, I will not hear. Your hands are full of blood. Wash yourselves, make yourselves clean; Put away the evil of your doings from before My eyes. Cease to do evil, Learn to do good…"Come now, and let us reason together," Says the LORD, " Though your sins are like scarlet, They shall be as white as snow; Though they are red like crimson, they shall be as wool" (Isaiah 1:11-18).

If we are disobedient we displease God. Right from the outset God made His expectations clear concerning obedience, 'Then Moses and the priests, who are Levites, said to all Israel, "Be silent, O Israel, and listen! You have now become the people of the LORD your God. Obey the LORD your God and follow his commands and decrees that I give you today" '(Deuteronomy 27:9-10). That is what God required of them and that is what God also requires of us; obedience to his revealed will. It is not enough to hear God's voice, we must obey. Obedience is part of the honour we owe God. God's Word tells us, "To obey is better than sacrifice" (1 Samuel 15:22).

The Old Testament King Saul thought it was enough for him to offer sacrifices though he disobeyed God's command. God rejected that sacrifice because obedience was lacking. God wants our worship but not if we are disobedient. Turning up to religious services and singing hymns is not pleasing to God unless we are walking in obedience to him. That's what empty religion is all about.

Our obedience must correspond with the Word of God. We can have traditions that are not related to the Word and that can get out of hand, as happened with the Pharisees. The apostle Paul advised the Colossians: 'Let no one cheat you of your reward, taking delight in *false* humility and worship of angels, intruding into those things which he has not seen, vainly puffed up by his fleshly mind (Colossians 2:18). Here Paul condemns the worship of angels which has a show of humility. Some people were loath to be so bold as to approach God directly. They would be more humble and prostrate themselves before the angels as mediators whom they believed would present their petitions to God. But this show of humility was hateful to God because it was not required in the Word. All that we do must be warranted by Scripture.

That is still done today by people who have a panoply of intermediaries which are called 'saints'. In an age of ecumenical endeavour it is considered wrong to criticise the dearly held religious convictions of other faiths. But if we are to please God we must look to His Word for guidance concerning the truth with regard to appropriate and acceptable forms of worship. There is much religion that is called 'Christian' but is in reality not biblical Christianity. I feel immensely sorry for people who are deceived by human traditions and thereby deprived of the truth.

There is a kind of obedience which is merely an external observance but this is not what God requires of us. What makes our obedience acceptable? Obedience must be free and cheerful. We might serve God with weakness but it must be with willingness. It is hypocrisy to obey God grudgingly. Cain brought his sacrifice but not his heart. God may accept your willingness even if you never get around to doing the work. But God will never accept your work without your willingness. Cheerfulness shows that there is love in the observance of the duty.

Our obedience must be earnest and fervent. James tells us, 'Elijah was a man with a nature like ours, and he prayed earnestly that it would not rain; and it did not rain on the land for three years and six months. And he prayed again, and the heaven gave rain, and the earth produced its fruit' (James 5:17-18). Elijah called for fire from heaven to consume the sacrifice on Mount Carmel and God sent the fire. He was vindicated, God was exalted and the prophets of Baal were destroyed and their god exposed as a sham. Elijah was fervent in spirit and his prayer opened and shut heaven. His prayer fetched fire from heaven but it also carried fire up to heaven.

Our obedience must be far-reaching and not limited. We must not obey God just in some things. We cannot be selective and choose the things that are easily achievable and of little worth. Herod would hear John the Baptist but not forsake his incestuous relationship. Many today are content to sit under the sound of preaching but they will not forsake their sins. We need to examine what we do and what we don't do. Some people pray but are very mean in giving to the Lord's work. Others are very generous but don't pray. We must not be selective in obeying God.

Our obedience must be sincere. Our aim must be the glory of God. Obedience is not just to satisfy our consciences and keep Jiminy Cricket quiet. Obedience is part of the process of becoming more like Jesus by being transformed into His likeness. And the end of that is to bring glory to God. This is what Scripture teaches, 'whatever you do, do all to the glory of God' (1 Corinthians 10:31). If our aims are wrong then our actions are useless. We may fall short in obedience but we should at least take aim at the target. The Pharisees gave alms but blew a trumpet about it because they wanted the glory.

The Old Testament character, Jehu, did well in destroying Baal worship and God commended him for it. But because his aims were not good (he aimed at settling himself in the kingdom) God looked on it as no better than murder. Thus we read in Hosea, "I will avenge the bloodshed of Jezreel on the house of Jehu" (1:4). There is a salutary lesson here, that we can fight battles for God and experience victories and still incur the displeasure of God.

We should not have an exaggerated view of what obedience might achieve because ultimately it is Christ's merit and not our obedience that makes us acceptable to God. To try to serve God in an attempt to procure favour with Him is more likely to provoke God than please Him. When King Uzziah offered incense without a priest God was angry with him and struck him down with leprosy (2 Chronicles 26:20). We must come to God through Christ because this is how we offer up the incense of worship. He is our priest.

Our obedience must be constant. The psalmist says, 'Blessed *are* those who keep justice, *and* he who does righteousness at all times!' (Psalm 106:3). Nobody is entirely consistent in always doing what is right but we are to aim to be constant in this regard. True obedience is like the fire on the altar that was always kept burning (Leviticus 6:13). We will encounter opposition and affliction but we must endeavour to be steady in our obedience. If we are to imitate Christ then remember that, 'He humbled Himself and became obedient to *the point of* death, even the death of the cross' (Philippians 2:8).

Many will not obey God. Many will not forsake their sins. It is quite astonishing to read in the Old Testament of those who refused to obey God:

> *"As for* the word that you have spoken to us in the name of the LORD, we will not listen to you! But we will certainly do whatever has gone out of our own mouth, to burn incense to the queen of heaven and pour out drink offerings to her, as we have done, we and our fathers, our kings and our princes, in the cities of Judah and in the streets of Jerusalem" (Jeremiah 44:16-17).

It is clear from this that they would not forsake their traditions even for God. They felt their traditions were sacred and refused to be corrected by God's Word. They preferred their customs and practices and would not conform to the clearly expressed Word of God. Does this sound familiar? There are many today who behave in exactly the same manner. They cherish their traditions and reject the Word of God. These people probably felt that Jeremiah was a crank or crackpot. To many people today the messengers of God appear to be halfwits with an idiotic message. But God will vindicate His

Word and woe to those who have spurned it in preference to their dearly held rites and rituals!

In what ways are we disobedient? We disobey when we know what our duty is and we do not do it. Disobedience comes not just from rebellion but also from ignorance. Do we know what God requires of us? Satan's strategy is to keep people in ignorance and unbelief. If he can keep people from knowing the mind of God and from believing the truth he can keep them from obeying it. Satan hates the Word of God. He hates the reading of it and he hates the preaching of it. Satan hates preachers and seeks to destroy them. Satan will whisper to believers, 'did God say?' Satan knows the Bible better than us and he will trick us if he can. Many obey the commands of the flesh rather than the commands of God.

Why should we obey God? Consider what the Scriptures say, "Now therefore, if you will indeed obey My voice and keep My covenant, then you shall be a special treasure to Me above all people; for all the earth *is* Mine" (Exodus 19:5) If we want to be the apple of his eye we must be obedient.

There is nothing lost by obedience. He is a friend and comforter and guide and there is blessing for those who obey. When we consider who God is, disobedience is irrational because it is foolish to defy God. It is destructive to disobey. Paul told the Thessalonians that a time would come: 'when the Lord Jesus is revealed from heaven with His mighty angels, in flaming fire taking vengeance on those who do not know God, and on those who do not obey the gospel of our Lord Jesus Christ' (2 Thessalonians 1:7-8).

God's commands are not unreasonable or burdensome but the commands of sin bring sorrow. Virtue is less demanding than vice. Many people are slaves to lust and the heartache it causes. God commands only what is beneficial to our souls and bodies. God told His people that the commands and decrees He issued and which He expected them to obey were for their own good (Deuteronomy 10:12-13). So to obey God is not a duty it is a privilege. We seem to think that obedience means foregoing the pleasures of sin. But God wants us to inherit the treasures of heaven; to find forgiveness for sin and freedom from guilt and damnation. There is love in every command.

God's Spirit makes obedience easy and delightful. In a passage that speaks of the renewal of Israel we read, "I will put My Spirit within you and cause you to walk in My statutes, and you will keep My judgments and do *them*" (Ezekiel 36:27). We should make that promise our prayer. The promise encourages us and the Spirit enables us to obey.

Love

Jesus summed up the law in one simple maxim:

> "The first of all the commandments *is: 'Hear, O Israel, the LORD our God, the LORD is one. And you shall love the LORD your God with all your heart, with all your soul, with all your mind, and with all your strength.'* This *is* the first commandment. And the second, like it, is this: *You shall love your neighbour as yourself.'* There is no other commandment greater than these." (Mark 12:29-31).

This echoes Deuteronomy, "You shall love the LORD your God with all your heart, with all your soul, and with all your strength" (6:5). The duty called for is love. Love for God is that holy fire which burns in our affections. Before we can love God we must know God. In relationship with Him we come to know His wisdom, holiness, power, mercy and grace. To adore God means to love Him intensely. It means to delight in Him as the object of our affections. The psalmist says, 'Delight yourself also in the LORD' (Psalm 37:4). Experiencing God's grace changes our aims and delights. The kind of love that God wants is whole-hearted not half-hearted love. The

Christian sometimes loves his sins more than God and his heart is divided in this way. But God does not want divided hearts.

We should love God for Himself and not to just seek the blessing but the One who blesses. It delighted me always whenever I returned home after a journey abroad that my children were glad to see me. They always looked into my face and not at my hands to see what gifts I might have brought for them. God wants us to seek His face and not His hands of blessing. This is a true test of our love for God. We should love Him for his intrinsic value; for who He is. He is excellent and altogether lovely. We are not to love the portion He gives more than the person He is. We get many blessings from God and that should certainly enhance our love as it proves His faithful character. But let us love Him for Himself and not just for what He gives.

We are to love God with all our might; as much as we are able. We can never love Him as much as he deserves. Our love for God should be vocal but more than that it should be active. An evident love is lived out for Him in ways that are real and demonstrable. Our minds should be focused on Him. Our hands should be busy for Him. Our feet should be walking in His ways. Scripture refers to this as a 'labour of love' (1 Thessalonians 1:3). All of our Christian endeavour should be prompted by love for God.

Mary Magdalene loved Jesus and poured expensive fragrant oil on Him. Others thought that was extravagant because they did not love like that. But she loved him and it seemed like the right thing to do. Love is extravagant. In love God is looking for the best; not what is good; not what is better but the best. God gave the best of His love when He gave Jesus. God wants to be first and foremost in our lives. He wants priority over everything else and everybody else. Is He our priority?

One of the fruits of the Holy Spirit is love. Where there are fruits there must be roots. If we really love God we will want to spend time with Him. We will want to abide in Him. When people are in love they naturally want to be together. If we love God we will never find contentment in anything without Him. Lovers cannot do without each other. If we love God we will hate whatever comes between us and Him. If we love God we share His sorrow at sin and we grieve for the things that grieve Him; as lovers do. The most certain evidence of our love for God is our obedience to His commands: '...this is the love of God, that we keep His commandments (1 John 5:3). This is what Jesus expects. He said, "If you love Me, keep My commandments" (John 14:15). If we love Him we will love His cause and we will work to promote His honour; to see Him esteemed among others.

If we admire His loveliness and if we are caught up in Him that will spill over and may even be contagious for others. I have a friend who is passionate about fishing (angling). I do not like fishing because I prefer to spend my time writing. But whenever I hear him talk about his hobby I want to go fishing with him. He is interesting on that topic because he is interested in it. Are we interested in God? Do we talk about God in such a way that people find it irresistible and want to know Him in the way we know Him? The girl who is in love is not silent about it. She will want to tell her friends about the one she loves. When lovers are apart they miss each other. They want to be close. If we love God we will want to be near to Him and to please Him.

It is a contradiction for someone to say he loves God if he habitually and flagrantly disobeys His commands. Many people profess to love God but they are not willing to suffer any loss for His sake. But if God loved us like that we would be lost.

How can we love God better? How can we know Him more? The Scriptures set forth His incomparable excellence and Jesus is the exact image of the Almighty. We see God's beauty and majesty in the person and work of Christ.

Love is like fire. Fire needs fuel and oxygen otherwise it can go out. We need to work at sustaining our passion for God. A fire can be quenched but God wants to fan into flame those dying embers of our love. John records what Jesus had to say to the church at Ephesus:

> "To the angel of the church of Ephesus write, 'These things says He who holds the seven stars in His right hand, who walks in the midst of the seven golden lamp-stands: "I know your works, your labour, your patience, and that you cannot bear those who are evil. And you have tested those who say they are apostles and are not, and have found them liars; and you have persevered and have patience, and have laboured for My name's sake and have not become weary. Nevertheless I have *this* against you, that you have left your first love. Remember therefore from where you have fallen; repent and do the first works, or else I will come to you quickly and remove your lamp-stand from its place — unless you repent" (Revelation 2:1-5).

Neglect of our spiritual duties, too much love for the world and preferring our ease and comfort to God's cause (the gospel) are signs of tepid love. The believers at Ephesus are commended for much but they are condemned for departing from the intensity of their first-love. First love is passionate and preoccupying.

When the law was given on Mount Sinai it was a terrifying experience in the history of Israel. The mountain burned with fire and billowed with smoke. The people at the foot of the mountain could hear the sound of a trumpet and words being spoken. Moses too was very afraid. The writer to the Hebrews contrasts this old covenant experience with the new covenant in Christ (Hebrews 12:1f.).

God has not changed but under the new covenant we come to realise that 'perfect love casts out fear' (1 John 4:18).

The law was given just three months after the children of Israel had been delivered from captivity in Egypt. They had lived under persecution but God, in His love, raised Moses up to mobilise a great exodus. This deliverance was marked by many miraculous events which demonstrated the power of God's great love for His people. God sent numerous plagues to demonstrate His power and to persuade Pharaoh to let His people go. We have already referred to the time when the Israelites were crossing the Red Sea on dry land in an effort to escape the pursuing Egyptian army. We have noted how God delivered them in a most extraordinary way when the walls of water on either side of them closed in on the Egyptians and they were drowned. These were frightening, amazing and memorable events. They had seen the might of God demonstrated in their lives. They had come to know their God as an awesome deliverer but behind all this activity and demonstration of power God's love was the motivating factor. So the giving of this law was an episode in the history of the people of Israel that they would never forget. This same law was repeated approximately forty years later as the children of Israel were about to enter the Promised Land (Deuteronomy 5).

It is interesting to note that when the apostle Paul (a former Pharisee of the tribe of Benjamin and one-time student of the great Gamaliel) lists the privileges of the Jews, he mentions the law amongst other benefits.

> For I could wish that I myself were accursed from Christ for my brethren, my countrymen according to the flesh, who are Israelites, to whom ***pertain*** the adoption, the glory, the covenants, the giving of the law, the service ***of God***, and the promises; of whom ***are*** the fathers and from whom, according to the flesh, Christ ***came***, who is over all, ***the*** eternally blessed God. Amen (Romans 9:3-5)

But the Hebrew people misunderstood the law because they came to see it as a step-ladder to enable them to climb up to heaven. This was a basic fallacy. The law is not a meritorious system whereby we can earn points or credits toward access to heaven. Nobody will get into heaven on this basis. The Torah contains approximately 630 regulations and as such it is an impossible standard.

Commands not Requests

We live in a secular and spiritual age of lawlessness where many Christians play fast and loose with the law of God. They recognise the truth that the Jews were confused about: that they can never justify themselves by keeping the law, but go on to draw the wrong conclusion that it does not matter, therefore, how they live. The attitude seems to be that it is good if you can keep the commandments but don't worry overmuch if you violate them. They say we all break them and Jesus died for our transgressions so all you have to do is ask for forgiveness and all will be well again. Sadly there is a mixture of truth and error in this kind of thinking with the result that the glory of the gospel is perverted.

We must seek to keep the law not just in an outward way but in an inward way. Law and grace are the two parameters that help us understand the message of the Bible. A dose of reverence and godly fear would not do any of us any harm. We flick a switch and we are in the worship mode. God is approachable but we ought not to be too casual in the manner of our approach. He is a majestic and powerful God who is not to be trifled with. God hates sin.

What is the law? It may seem like a tautological statement to say that the commandments are commands, but it needs to be stated. In any civilised country there are laws. These are not pieces of advice presented for our consideration. All residents, citizens and guests of the nation must abide by the laws in place within any given territory or face the consequences. The commandments are not just wisdom accumulated over a period of time and offered to us on a take-it-or-leave-it basis. God is not saying, "it would be nice if you adhered to these recommendations." The law of God, like the law of the land comes with authority and in essence has an imperative tone. There is something urgent and obligatory about the law. Behind the commandments there is supreme authority.

In the first epistle of John we have a definition of sin, 'Whoever commits sin also commits lawlessness, and sin is lawlessness' (3:4). God gave us the law so that we might know the difference between right and wrong and thereby assist us in knowing what we should and should not do. It is wrong to think of the commandments as a custom. Certain sins may have social consequences but sin is not just a breach of social custom, it is an offence to God. Customs are relative to time, place and certain groups of people. There is nothing absolute about custom. For example in Western society black is the colour for mourning but in Korea white is the acceptable colour for mourning.

In an age of pluralism and postmodernism morality is relative. So that what one person deems to be wrong may well be thought to be perfectly right in another person's thinking. There is no consensus about many moral and ethical issues. But God is absolute and His Word is the final authority in all matters of faith and practice. He expects us to pay heed to it. It is not just kindly, fatherly advice whereby He is saying, "live in this way and things will work out well for you and you will be happier" (though that will be the outcome). These are commands to be obeyed.

In Western culture there is a crisis of authority which is manifest on the streets at night and in the schools by day. People resent authority and reject discipline. People don't like to be told what to do. People don't like to be told that their behaviour is wrong. But God's laws are a blessing. Imagine what our society would be like if these were obeyed. It would be heaven on earth.

Flee to Jesus

Jesus had trouble, not with the people who were contemptuously and disparagingly referred to as 'sinners', but with Scribes and Pharisees. These were the religious leaders and teachers of the law! They were the people who poured over the Torah and specialised in explaining it and enforcing it. They were constantly waiting to pounce on Jesus if He put a foot wrong. When Jesus healed on the Sabbath they were annoyed with what they perceived to be a breach of the Sabbath. They hated Him because He attacked the notion that they could use the commandments as a means of salvation.

We have already seen how Paul told the Galatians that the law is our schoolmaster to bring us to Christ. The commandments show us that we have violated God's law not just in outward detail but in inward principle. There is a staggering statement in the Sermon on the Mount where Jesus teaches that to look at a woman with lust is adultery.[2] True Christianity teaches that to harbour hatred in your heart is tantamount to murder. This is strong stuff! In teaching like this Jesus was effectively teaching the Pharisees that their observance was external and that it was essentially impossible to keep the law. They saw the law as just about outward actions but Jesus taught that the law was also about inward motives and thoughts. Their hope of salvation was based on their self-effort but Christ disabused them of such false notions and they disliked Him and His message.

---

[2] This is further elaborated in the seventh chapter.

Jesus was not saying, "relax: don't worry about the law because you haven't a hope of keeping it anyway". Rather He was saying the law should turn us to God for mercy and grace. In this way Jesus shows us the true nature of the law. The law convicts and convinces of sin. Before sinners turn to Jesus they have to see a reason and will not see it unless they are first convinced of their sinful condition and sense the guilt of that.

God gave us these Commandments that we might know His will and to know when we have violated His will. The law teaches us to flee to Jesus for refuge and forgiveness.

And was it for my sin

And was it for my sin
That Jesus suffered so,
When moved by His all-powerful love
He came to earth below.

Thy holy law fulfilled,
Atonement now is made,
And our great debt, too great for us,
He now has fully paid.

He suffered pain and death,
When on the hill brought low;
His blood will wash the guilty clean,
As pure and white as snow.

For in His death our death
Died with Him on the tree,
And a great number by His blood
Will go to heaven made free.

When Jesus bowed His head
And dying took our place,
The veil was rent, a way was found
To that pure home of grace.

He conquered blackest hell;
He trod the serpent down;
A host from fetters He'll set free
By grace to be God's own.[3]

The First Commandment

You shall have no other Gods before Me

The first commandment says, "You shall have no other gods before Me." What does God want us to know by this statement? What does this statement require of us? It requires us to know and acknowledge God as the only true God. It demands that we acknowledge Him as our God and worship and glorify Him accordingly.

It clearly forbids us to deny the existence of God. The Bible does not seek to prove the existence of God. Rather it asserts that knowledge of His existence is built into the innate consciousness of all people. Modern man thinks it is clever to be an atheist and some people look on believers with pity and contempt. But the Bible says, 'The fool has said in his heart, " *There is* no God" ' (Psalm 14:1). The New Testament says that people who deny the existence of God are without excuse, 'For since the creation of the world His invisible *attributes* are clearly seen, being understood by the things that are made, *even* His eternal power and Godhead, so that they are without excuse' (Romans 1:20). People are under an obligation to worship and serve Him.

The God who spoke these words was the Hebrew God Jehovah; the One with whom Jesus was equal in status: "I and My Father are one" (John 10:30). He was distinct from other 'gods' of the time. He is not just a local tribal deity. He is the one true God. He is the universal God. There is no other God. Scripture speaks of God in personal terms; not just as a supreme being or as the great architect of the universe. Though He is all that. We are not dealing with an abstract proposition or figment of people's imaginations. We are dealing with a living God; a person who speaks. Scripture is His Word.

The essence of this commandment is that we should sanctify God in our hearts and give him precedence above everything else. Is God our God? We are to be persuaded in our hearts that He is God. We are to proclaim this with our lips and live out that acknowledgment in practical ways. God calls us to acknowledge Him and follow Him. God calls us to honour Him in our lives and worship Him. We, like Joshua in the Old Testament, need to make that decision and make that decision known to others:

> "And if it seems evil to you to serve the LORD, choose for yourselves this day whom you will serve, whether the gods which your fathers served that *w ere* on the other side of the River, or the gods of the Amorites, in whose land you dwell. But as for me and my house, we will serve the LORD." So the people answered and said: "Far be it from us that we should forsake the LORD to serve other gods; for the LORD our God *is* He who brought us and our fathers up out of the land of Egypt, from the house of bondage, who did those great signs in our sight, and preserved us in all the way that we went and among all the people through whom we passed" (Joshua 24:15-18).

Clearly Joshua's knowledge of God was based on real experience of Him. It is one thing to acknowledge the truth of this intellectually but another thing altogether to choose Him. This truth must also engage the will. It is not a matter of chance it is a matter of choice. Before choosing him there must be knowledge of Him. We must recognize that He is the Almighty and that we are His creation. He is our superior and we are His subordinates. The commandments begin with God because He is to be first and foremost in our lives. God is essentially saying, "Put first things first". He is making it clear that our understanding of Him; His power and position matter. The commandments don't begin with morality and the gospel does not begin with morality; it begins with God. The commandments teach us that there is no hope for society unless and until it is right with God. That is where the code begins. The commandments are like a series of numbers in a combination lock. Without the first digit the lock will not open. Man's fundamental trouble is that he has trouble between himself and God. People have become estranged from God. True religion and true morality begin with God and the very order of the commandments drives that point home.

Biblically Minded

The refrain of Isaiah 45 is, "I *am* the LORD, and *there is* no other...*there is* no God besides Me...*There is* no other God". In that portion of Scripture God says: "...I have made the earth, and created man on it...My hands—stretched out the heavens, and all their host I have commanded..." (v.12). These words were spoken into a society that was familiar with the idea of many gods. The first commandment is relevant today. We assert that there is one God and that Jesus is the only way to heaven as Peter proclaimed, "there is no other name under heaven given among men by which we must be saved" (Acts 4:12). To hold this view in a pluralist and postmodern society is deemed to be narrow-minded. But is it not to be biblically minded?

This particular Christian view flies in the face of the inter-faith agenda and is extremely unpopular. In this regard first-century Christians and twenty-first-century Christians are alike. Both are thought to be dogmatic and extreme. Many people who call themselves Christians have abandoned the unique and universal claims of Christ. The Old Testament Jews were also thought to be exclusivist and uncompromising and were held in contempt by others. First-century Christians were martyred by the Roman authorities, not because they believed in Jesus but because they refused to give allegiance to other 'gods', including Caesar. This was deemed to be arrogant and treasonous. Christians today who uphold the teaching of Christ who said, "I am the way, the truth, and the life. No one comes to the Father except through Me" (John 14:6) are despised and rejected. They are objects of scorn and are ridiculed and pilloried for their faith.

Throughout the centuries many missionaries went to societies that were religious or pagan and laid down their lives for the gospel. They did not go to irreligious societies, they went to places that had their own deities and said that Jesus was the only way. Many are still engaged in clandestine missionary activity in parts of the world where this message is deemed to be sacrilegious and treasonous and punishable by imprisonment, flogging or even by death. The whole rationale of the Christian missionary enterprise in history has operated on the premise that, "there is no other name under heaven given among men by which we must be saved". Many missionaries have been killed for disseminating this message. Their lives were wasted if Jesus is not the only way to heaven.

People say that religious intolerance causes civil disruption and so we must legislate against it.[1] Some people would probably like to

---

[1] There has been in recent years a minority of Muslim preachers who incited other people to hatred and violence and it is necessary to have some laws to deal with such extreme cases.

gag Christians and not allow them make such unique and universal claims for Christ. The spirit of the age is 'tolerance' so that we can live harmoniously in the new millennium. But few are prepared to tolerate what they perceive to be the claims of diehards, fundamentalists and fanatics. But Christians are not inciting violence and recruiting zealots for terrorist campaigns. Tolerance is not a virtue in the same way as loyalty is not a virtue. People can be tolerant of evil and loyal to people and causes that are wrong, such as prevailed in Nazi Germany in the 1930's and 1940's and such as still exists in neo-Nazi groups today.

God says, "You shall have no other gods before Me" but pressure to conform to the spirit of the age has caused some believers to modify their message so that it fits in with the prevailing culture. In proclaiming the gospel Christians are merely proclaiming what the Bible teaches, *'there is* one God and one Mediator between God and men, *the* Man Christ Jesus' (1 Timothy 2:5).

Christians exist in multi-cultural and multi faith societies. It is right that there should be tolerance of other mainstream and minority religions. We must respect those who hold alternative religious views and work toward a society where freedom of conscience is accommodated. Non-Christian religions have the right to exist and the right to express their views and they should be allowed to worship in accordance with their customs and traditions. In fact we would desire to see this liberty extended to Christians in other countries, particularly in the Muslim world. But that does not mean that Christians should accept the veracity of their beliefs. We are entitled to hold biblically informed views about what they believe and we are entitled to express them. But we should always endeavour to express the truth in love. Whenever we do so without love we fail to represent Christ properly and, potentially, generate hostility.

We cannot be willing to say that all religions are equally valid. So, to take part in a multi-faith service, for example, would be a total denial of the gospel. There is no point in saying we are there to represent evangelical Christianity. We cannot line ourselves up with people who pray to another God. We cannot go through the charade of worship when what the man of another religion is saying is a lie. No matter how nice the person is and no matter how well-intentioned we or they may be. If all roads lead to heaven who is the majority who are going to hell? Jesus said, "…wide is the gate and broad is the way that leads to destruction, and there are many who go in by it. Because narrow is the gate and difficult is the way which leads to life, and there are few who find it" (Matthew 7:13-14). Jesus is the way! Do you think He didn't offend when He said that? The Hindu going to the Ganges to purify himself in ritual washing is a poor deluded soul. To say that what he believes is on an equal footing is a cruel deceit.

Do you believe the first commandment and are you willing to say it? It is not now nor has it ever been politically correct to make such an assertion. It is as unpopular now as it has always been. Prince Charles (the Prince of Wales) said some years ago[2] that if/when he became king he would like to be regarded not as the defender of *the* faith but as the defender of faith. He was really saying that in multi-cultural and multi-religious Britain who is to say that other faiths are wrong and Christianity is right. But that is a violation of the first commandment. Some might argue that it is a good thing that people

---

[2] This is a matter of public record and I believe the words were spoken in 1998 or 1999.

find faith in a secular age. But it is important not to have misplaced faith.

When we are driving along the road and get a puncture we are sure to place the car-jack on solid ground so that it can do its work effectively. If we were to place the jack on the soft margin all the energy and effort expended in hoisting it would be in vain because the jack would sink into the soft soil. The car-jack is like our faith: we must place it on solid ground or it is futile. Jesus is unique. He is the rock on whom our faith and trust depend. Though He has many rivals He has no peer. All routes do not lead to salvation. Christianity is not merely one of the options that you can take should you fancy that sort of thing!

How do we apply this commandment in our society? It does not mean that we can be churlish, mean, contemptuous, dismissive or rude to the devotees of other religions. We don't burn Mosques, smash statues, destroy shrines and grottos or ridicule people of other religions. They are entitled to freedom of conscience; even though that freedom is not afforded to Christianity in other countries. But we desire it. We are free to speak to them and win them. We are not bigots and we are not narrow-minded but we are people of conviction and it is out of a sense of genuine compassion for the eternal welfare of their souls that we share the gospel. We need wisdom and we should always be courteous and humble and firm. We should know the Word of God and be careful to explain from the Word. But we should smash the false gods in our own lives. What is on the throne of our minds is what dominates our thinking. What is on the throne of our hearts is what controls our affections.

Hey You!

This commandment speaks directly to individuals. Our attitude should be that what God says is more important than what others think. We should be prepared to accept what He has revealed. It is possible to have another person who takes that place of pre-eminence in our lives and in a sense that person is our god. It is possible that we have a hobby which usurps God from the place which is rightfully His. It is possible to have a career that is our God. There are many things that can be substitutes for God in our lives or displace Him from that foremost position in our affections. We might well ask where does God fit into our lives and to what extent we are observing this first commandment, "You shall have no other gods before Me". May the one true God dominate our minds and control our affections so that our wills become compliant with His sovereign purposes. It is one thing to have God in our minds but quite another to have Him as the God of our minds. We can have God in our affections but is He the God of our affections? We can bemoan the fact that this commandment is flagrantly violated in society but we must be careful that it is observed in our own lives.

But we might say God is a bit abstract for such a place in our lives. We have a husband, a wife, children, pets, homes, gardens, cars, caravans, boats, careers, hobbies and friends. All of these people and things take our time and energy and we will give God one hour on Sunday. But surely we can honour the Lord in our thoughts, words and deeds in all our human relationships and in all our responsibilities. If we revere Him in our hearts and esteem Him in our minds and speak to Him and of Him then Sunday worship time becomes the hour we look forward to. It is the quality time for which we have longed throughout the week.

There is much to distract our attention from God, especially in the busy world of today but it is one thing to be distracted and quite another thing to allow God to be displaced from that place of honour which is rightly His. Let us acknowledge God as God in all we say and do and think. He is jealous of our affections and desires to be enthroned in our lives.

When God says, "You shall have no other gods before Me", He is telling us not to engage in idolatrous practices. We don't have to participate in strange religious rites and rituals in order to be guilty of idolatry. When God becomes the least of our priorities and we allocate last place to Him then we have offended Him and we have broken this first commandment, "You shall have no other gods before Me". May God fill our being, control our passions and determine our ways.

God be in my head,

And in my understanding ;

God be in mine eyes,

And in my looking;

God be in my mouth,

And in my speaking;

God be in my heart,

And in my thinking;

God be at mine end,

And at my departing.[3]

---

[3] *Book of Hours*, 1514.

The Second Commandment

You shall not make for yourself a
carved image – any likeness of anything
that is in heaven above, or that is in the earth
beneath, or that is in the water under the earth;
you shall not bow down to them nor
serve them. For I, the LORD your God,
am a jealous God, visiting the iniquity of the
fathers upon the children to the third and
fourth generations of those who hate Me,
but showing mercy to thousands, to those who
love Me and keep My commandments

This second commandment is a warning against idolatry. It is the second longest of the commandments (the fourth, concerning Sabbath observance is the longest). Here the Lord makes His expectations very clear. He leaves us in no doubt about what is unacceptable and He emphasises the dire consequences that will ensue to those who deviate in this matter.

When Moses came down from Sinai the children of Israel were doing the very thing that God had forbidden. Aaron, the brother of Moses and a leader of the people was involved, along with God's people, in idol worship. They had made a golden calf and were worshipping it. So Moses returned to a terrible scene of vice and ungodliness. He had been away for approximately six weeks and in that short space of time the people had descended into apostasy. This is all the more extraordinary in the light of the fact that they were a people who had experienced the might and majestic power of God.

This commandment follows naturally from the first, 'You shall have no other gods before Me'. This passage (Exodus 32) indicates that there is something very powerful about idolatry; that the human heart naturally turns to it. Idolatry is, obviously, about the worship of idols but less obviously it is about inappropriate devotion to a person or thing which acts as a substitute for God. We may not bow down in front of idols and yet be guilty of idolatry when we venerate or love something excessively.

We might be inclined to think that idolatry is something that happens only in primitive societies. We may think that it is a practice consigned to history and that in this enlightened day and age it doesn't happen anymore. But this is very naïve. There is much idolatry in the world today. Often it is dressed up as something else. Religious systems that incorporate statues and icons are inherently idolatrous.

There is a tendency to think that this commandment is far removed from our experience. We don't have idols at home or in church. We can see how relevant it was to the children of Israel but cannot see how it might relate to us. But we are wrong! Idolatry was the besetting sin of Israel and it led to their Egyptian and Babylonian captivity. Right throughout the Old Testament it is evident. But by the New Testament period the Jews were different. Their art and architecture contained no visual images or statues. This is borne out by archaeological excavations which show that other contemporary civilisations had an abundance of such things. Museums and art galleries around the world are packed with Greek and Roman statues but not Jewish.

Scripture is verbal not visual. This commandment does not forbid painting, sculpture, visual and graphic art. But it clearly forbids the misuse of images and this includes their use in worship. There is virtually no physical description of Jesus given in the New Testament. We might well ask why? Novels give physical descriptions but the New Testament does not give such details about Jesus.

Exodus 32 records the crude version of idolatry. What makes it appalling is the fact that it is indulged not by heathen but by God's people. They literally melted down their jewellery and made a golden calf. This kind of crass activity is still practiced in many parts of the world today. Totem poles are carved from trees and were once worshipped. For some people today they are a relatively popular and innocuous item of curiosity or part of their home décor. But they have a peculiar history.

So too do charm bracelets. Some years ago charm bracelets were popular. Ladies in the 1950s and 1960s collected charms. These were bracelets worn around the wrist with personal charms, decorative pendants or trinkets that signified important things or events in the wearer's life.

Although their popularity waned through the latter part of the twentieth-century, there was a resurgence of interest after 2000 and collectors eagerly sought out vintage charms. Due to the movie *Pirates of the Caribbean*, the fashion in winter 2006 was bracelets with little charms of swords, crosses and skulls.

For most people they are just items of jewellery or fashion accessories but the wearing of charms probably began as a form of amulet to ward off evil spirits or bad luck. In ancient Egypt charms were used for identification and as symbols of faith and luck. Charms also served to identify an individual to the gods in the afterlife. Medieval knights wore charms for protection in battle. Although sanitised by time they too (like totem poles) have a peculiar history and I would not want to purchase one.

The Bible teaches that God made man in His image but men are inclined to make their own gods in various images. But idolatry does not always come in that form. In considering the first commandment we established that a person or thing may take the place of God and so displace and usurp Him. We identified there what those things might be, so suffice it to say at this point that ambition, family, friends, material possessions, career, self-advancement, sex, ideologies, political allegiances, hobbies and a host of other things can supersede God in our affections. Heroes of history can come to be idolised in our thinking and so too certain places can take on a spiritual significance in the imaginations of people. Anything that is more important to us than God is an idol. The Apostle Paul's letter to the Colossians says that covetousness[1] is idolatry, 'Therefore put to death…fornication, uncleanness, passion, evil desire, and covetousness, which is idolatry' (Colossians 3:5).

False Notions

The second commandment is a warning to us not to engage in idolatry. Idolatry is at war with faith. In heaven we won't need faith because we will have sight of Jesus. The idolater says that faith is not enough, he needs an object. But the way of salvation is by faith. We don't need to bolster faith with tangible, physical things. Faith does not depend on sight. Faith is superior to sight.

---

[1] This point will be further developed in the tenth chapter.

But we also need to be careful about our idea of God because we can break this commandment by having a false God that does not match the true God of the Bible. We can have mental images of God which are not based on the Word. Some people don't like the image of God presented in Scripture so they make their own God. These people are as much idolaters as the crude and crass literalist who bows down to an image of 'god'.

We have to come back to the Bible and ask; who is God? What is God like? How is He to be worshipped? The God of the Bible is to be our God. How can God the Father be depicted? How can God the Holy Spirit be depicted? How can Jesus be depicted? That which is spiritual cannot be depicted in physical form.

However imaginatively Jesus is depicted it is merely a guess at what is only His human appearance. If the *Turin Shroud* was an authentic artefact, which depicts the face of Christ in silhouette form, it would be of some historical value but would have no spiritual significance. We don't need pictorial representation when we have faith in Jesus.

If we want to worship God in a way that pleases Him then the first commandment tells us about the correct God to worship and the second commandment tells us about how that correct God is to be worshipped correctly. The obvious and immediate intent of the commandment is to teach people to avoid idolatry. But there is another application because this commandment touches the theme of worship.

True Worship

God underlines the message of this commandment so that in addition to the commandment being stated there are words of additional warning and promise. This extra emphasis underscores the importance of the message. It is as if God is saying: "before you move on; before you skip through the list make sure you thoroughly understand the gravity and seriousness of what I'm saying here."

God describes Himself as a jealous God. Jealousy is usually an evil thing that says something about a person's bad character. But there are proper areas in which a person should be jealous. People should jealously guard their reputations and honour. Any violation of these things should arouse a righteous jealousy. God has a righteous jealousy and promises to punish those who violate this commandment and bless those who observe it:

> "For I, the LORD your God, *am* a jealous God, visiting the iniquity of the fathers upon the children to the third and fourth *generations* of those who hate Me, but showing mercy to thousands, to those who love Me and keep My commandments."

The sins perpetrated in one generation may be perpetuated in subsequent generations. This is one of the social consequences of sin. There is nothing arbitrary or unfair in God. One generation's sins cause trouble for the next generation. When the father is a criminal in the family the children may be raised in an environment which is conducive to criminal activity. If the father is a drug dealer the son can get involved and continue the illegitimate business. In this way the family is cursed, not by God but by their own commitment to sinful activity. The son need not, necessarily, become involved in the subterranean world of the father. God can (and does) break into such situations. Criminals are converted and pass on entirely different values to their children. Thus a godly influence in one generation of a family can be the start of a great heritage and lead to tremendous blessing in subsequent generations. The additional comment in this commandment adds a great solemnity to it.

This commandment draws us into the theme of worship. The first commandment tells us not to worship false gods but the second commandment tells us not to worship the true God in a false way. That is an abomination to God. Are we innocent of transgressing this commandment? In order to answer that question we must first ask: how is God to be worshipped and how is God not to be worshipped? As we come to God we should prepare our hearts. We can prepare by meditating on the things of God?

When we are in church are we itching for the service to finish? Do we want to get the God slot out of the way as quickly as possible? When the service is over do you switch off the religion and turn on the secular channel? Some churches depart after the service because they don't want that sense of God to evaporate. There is a downside to this but the principle is commendable. Do you ever turn off T.V. after a lovely programme because you don't want to spoil the mood? You want to savour it.

How is God to be worshipped? The Bible gives full testimony to the fact that God is a speaking God. That is why in our services we read the Word and have preaching. We give priority to what is spoken rather than what is seen. God is not just a speaking God but He is a communicating God. This is a two-way process. We look to Him to speak to us and He looks to us to speak to Him. So we pray and sing hymns of prayer and praise.

Distractions

The history of church buildings is interesting. There were none in the New Testament. Believers met in the precincts of the temple court in Jerusalem. These were open courts and colonnades where Christians were able to gather in their thousands. As the gospel spread across the Near East they began to meet in peoples homes or sometimes they hired a hall. After some years they began to have buildings. These were simple types of structures initially. After a time the structures changed. They were based on the Roman architectural style of basilicas with a large domed area. As the centuries went on they became more and more elaborate, reflecting a theological architecture. In the Medieval period there were very ornate churches. Cathedrals are meant to reflect something of the grandeur of God.

From one point of view these buildings are very beautiful as architecture, aesthetically magnificent and historically significant. But they also tell us something about worship. They have the potential to distract from the true worship of God. During the Reformation the pulpit (which had been consigned to an off-centre position in church buildings) became central again as did the Lord's Table; not as an altar but as a table of remembrance. Non conformists had meeting houses. In the nineteenth-century a Gothic revival was led by some people who regretted the Reformation and tried to go back to a point before the Reformation. They built very elaborate and expensive churches in a gothic style and the simplicity of worship was lost.

With regard to liturgy it is clear that the further away you come from the purity of the Bible the more elaborate the service becomes, with processions, pomp and ceremony. But this is very far removed from the New Testament. In many instances music changed because ordinary people were not deemed to be good enough and so choirs were introduced to professionalize the sound. The function of a choir should be to lead the congregation in worship, not to put on a performance. There is a place for choirs performing in a worship service but not to the exclusion of congregational singing. We don't want to admire the choir any more than the preacher. When people heard Joseph Parker (a contemporary of Spurgeon) preach they said, "What a preacher!" but when people heard Spurgeon preach they said, "What a saviour!" The Bible does not speak about the holiness of beauty; rather it speaks about the beauty of holiness. This second commandment gives us much food for thought.

The Present Situation

The whole concept of worship today has been debased. What is legitimate? Does anything go? It isn't good enough to say, "I like it and my friends like it". We don't begin with what we like; we begin with what God likes. What does He want us to do? Many churches operate on a user-friendly basis. Of course we should be friendly but there is something wrong with going to the world and asking, "What kind of church would you like?" Yet this market research approach is popular. We should never conduct a poll of people in the locality and ask, "What would you like?" Can you imagine Jesus operating on that principle? Our primary concern should be to please God and to find out what He wants.

Politicians are despised because they don't lead by conviction and principle any more. There are very few ideologically driven politicians. They have focus groups to identify what people want and then they serve that up in their manifestos. Imagine if we were to write our church constitution like that.

Idolising Tradition

In this commandment God is concerned about how He should be worshipped. Over time things that are harmless and innocuous acquire a degree of symbolism and devotion and they have to be got rid of. Numbers 21 recounts the story of the plague of serpents which afflicted God's people in the wilderness. It tells of the act of God's mercy in providing the bronze serpent hoisted up on a pole for all to see. Those who looked to this lived. But that snake was kept through the centuries until a king called Hezekiah came to the throne:

> Now it came to pass...*that* Hezekiah...began to reign...he did *w h at w a s* right in the sight of the LORD...He removed the high places and broke the *sacred* pillars, cut down the wooden image and broke in pieces the bronze serpent that Moses had made; for

until those days the children of Israel burned incense to it, and called it Nehushtan (2 Kings 18:1-4).

It diverted from the true worship of God. The principle that guided Hezekiah was the second commandment. We need to be careful that our traditions don't take on a sanctity that makes them sacrilegious.

The Third Commandment

You shall not take the name of the LORD your God in vain, for the LORD will not hold him guiltless who takes His name in vain

God's name and nature are inextricably connected. God revealed Himself to Moses as compassionate, gracious, patient, loving, faithful, and forgiving. But He also disclosed that He is a righteous judge who will not let sin go unpunished.

Jesus condescended to leave the glory of heaven and take on human form. But now He is once again exalted to the highest place. Paul tells the Philippians that Jesus is, 'the name which is above every name' (Philippians 2:9). He goes on to tell them, 'that at the name of Jesus every knee should bow, of those in heaven, and of those on earth, and of those under the earth, and *that* every tongue should confess that Jesus Christ *is* Lord, to the glory of God the Father (Philippians 2:10-11).

Question 54 of the catechism asks: 'What is required of the third commandment?' The answer is given: 'The third commandment requires the holy and reverent use of God's names, titles, attributes, ordinances, word and works'. God is to be spoken of reverently.

David says, 'Give unto the LORD the glory due to His name' (Psalm 29:2). We are to ascribe to the Lord the honour that He rightly deserves. In another psalm he said, 'I will worship toward Your holy temple, and praise Your name' (Psalm 138:2). This is the believer's duty and joy.

But there is a great deal of disrespect for the name of God in today's society. The name of Jesus is often profaned in public. The precious name is just a swear word for many. On the radio in Ireland 'Jesus' is not bleeped over, like the 'F' word is. This third commandment expressly forbids the profaning of that precious name. But it is a name which is commonly abused. Isaiah speaks of truth in the gutter when he says, 'truth is fallen in the street' (Isaiah 59:14). Jesus is the truth, traduced.

It seems that people can profane with impunity but this commandment warns that the Lord will hold people accountable in this regard. Deuteronomy 28 lists curses which will befall those who are disobedient to God's commands. In that chapter it says, "…that you may fear this glorious and awesome name, THE LORD YOUR GOD' (v.58). If the people were not to be dispossessed they were to have due honour for the name of God. They were to have a reverential awe for that sacred name and all that it represents to them as creator, redeemer, provider and protector.

As Christians we bear Christ's noble name and so we must endeavour not to bring dishonour on it. If we fail and bring His name into disrepute we can have forgiveness but let us do all we can to promote the honour of His name in our communities. What a wonderful name Jesus is. An angel of the Lord appeared to Joseph, who was to be the future foster-father of Jesus, and said:

> "And she [Mary] will bring forth a Son, and you shall call His
> name JESUS, for He will save His people from their sins" So all
> this was done that it might be fulfilled which was spoken by the
> Lord through the prophet, saying: ***"Behold, the virgin shall be with
> child, and bear a Son, and they shall call His name Immanuel,"*** which is
> translated, "God with us" (Matthew 1:21-23).

That is the significance of the name Jesus. He is the Saviour.

In the Lord's Prayer we say, 'hallowed be Your name'. But the
tongue is an unruly member and needs to be disciplined because our
base natures are prone to profanity. James spoke of the tongue as
an important organ of the body. He said horses are steered by a bit
in their mouths and ships are steered by their rudders and the life is
steered by the tongue. Our words can be like sparks that start forest
fires. He speaks of the tongue as unruly and evil and full of deadly
poison and says, 'Out of the same mouth come praise and cursing'
(James 3:10).

People are careful to protect the honour of their names and
will go to court in cases of libel and defamation to defend their
reputations. There will, one day, be a court hearing where the name
of Jesus will be exonerated and every knee will bow and every tongue
will confess that Jesus is Lord.

I once met the American ambassador to Ireland and I addressed
her as she is accustomed and entitled to be addressed, "Your
Excellency". In doing this I was showing due reverence for the office
and person of the ambassador. She represented a great nation and
to slight her or be offensive or rude to her would have been
tantamount to dishonouring the nation she represented. Jesus is God
and to nonchalantly swear is to violate all that God is and it offends
that far country we call heaven.

It is astonishing that Christian complaints to the media (radio and television) about the abuse of the Lord's name are largely ignored in Ireland. Radio stations seem to think it is cool to swear. They have a callous disregard for the sensibilities of believers who find it profoundly offensive. To say that it is only a habit is no excuse. It is a very bad habit. If they used the 'C' word all decent people would be outraged. They don't use it because they know they won't get away with it. I don't hear them using the name of Mohammad or Allah in the same way! These people think Christians are weird and they see us as Mary Whitehouse types. But we are ordinary people who love God and worship Jesus and their attitude to Christians is second only to their obnoxious attitude to Christ.[1]

Lips and Lives

The name of Jesus is incomparably excellent but when we worship Him with our lips only we use His name in vain. The book of Isaiah noted that the people of God were hypocritical in their worship. They said the right words but they were devoid of sincerity, 'these people draw near with their mouths and honour Me with their lips, but have removed their hearts far from Me' (Isaiah 29:13). We profane His name when we call Him Lord but He is not Lord in our lives. We speak ill of God when we murmur at His providence and question His will and ways.

Great Titles

Isaiah, speaking prophetically of the messiah said, 'His name will be called Wonderful, Counsellor, Mighty God, Everlasting Father, Prince of Peace (Isaiah 9:6). Jesus was wonderful in His birth. Jesus was

---

[1] I would not wish to convey the idea that I think all Irish radio D. J. presenters and chat show hosts are vulgar. This is not the case.

wonderful in His life. Jesus was wonderful in His death. Is Jesus wonderful to us? If we trust Him we too will find Him wonderful.

As counsellor He became available, with answers to life's ultimate questions. As counsellor He brought assurance of salvation and sins forgiven to all who called upon His name and repented of their sins. Is He our counsellor? Does the Word of God guide and govern our lives? He is available to us with heavenly wisdom. If we bring our burdens and problems to Him then He will guide us. He is the Mighty God:

> Who has measured the waters in the hollow of His hand, measured heaven with a span and calculated the dust of the earth in a measure? Weighed the mountains in scales and the hills in a balance? Behold, the nations *are* as a drop in a bucket, and are counted as the small dust on the scales; look, He lifts up the isles as a very little thing. And Lebanon *is* not sufficient to burn, nor its beasts sufficient for a burnt offering. All nations before Him *are* as nothing… (Isaiah 40:12f.).

We can prove that might in our lives. We can trust in His strength day by day and in doing so we honour His name. We honour His name when we proclaim that He is mighty to save. We honour His name when we believe and declare that He is mighty to solve our problems. We can trust in His strength.

He is the everlasting one who entered time and space and made Himself subject to time so that we the subjects of time could be offered everlasting life. We should receive this gift while there is still time.

He is the Prince of Peace. We can be at peace with God when our sins are forgiven and we are walking in newness of life. We can experience the peace of God which comes from that new and dynamic relationship with Him. Many long for peace today. Christ can bring peace that passes all understanding to troubled hearts. These are just a few of the amazing titles for God but they give us a glimpse of his nature.

Denial and Dishonour

We are to honour His name and that starts with acknowledging who He is. Although it is common in society, to disparage the name of God by denying His existence it is something not taken lightly by God. To deny Him as creator is to dishonour His name. To reject Him as Saviour is to dishonour His name. To deny His omnipotence is to dishonour His name. To deny His omniscience is to dishonour His name. To deny His benevolence is to dishonour His name. To use that name irreverently or lightly or to abuse it is a serious matter for which God will hold people accountable.

It is not that this was just an instruction for the Hebrew nation at that time. We have dealt with that and shown that this commandment is for all peoples of all nations in all ages. It is not the ceremonial law which has passed away. It is not the judicial law which related to the specific cultural context of a previous time. It is the abiding and universal law of God. It is sacred.

It grieves the Holy Spirit when the name of God is profaned. It should grieve us more to hear it profaned. We should never get used to it. We should never dismiss it as merely a bad habit that people have. We should never treat it lightly because God has said that He will not let the matter go unpunished.

The commandments of God are becoming increasingly marginalised in a society which deems them to be irrelevant. Christ's name is abused by those who deny His deity and say He was merely a good man, a good teacher or a prophet of God. Many take the name of Jesus in vain but those who call on Him for salvation will not find their words of regret and repentance to have been in vain.

God keeps His promises. Those who wilfully and habitually profane His great name will be cursed. But those who honour His name will be blessed.

The Fourth Commandment

Remember the Sabbath day, to keep it holy.
Six days you shall labour and do all your work,
but the seventh day is the Sabbath of the LORD
your God. In it you shall do no work: you, nor
your son, nor your daughter,
nor your male servant, nor your female
servant, nor your cattle, nor your stranger who
is within your gates. For in six days
the LORD made the heavens and the earth, the
sea, and all that is in them, and rested
the seventh day. Therefore the LORD blessed the
Sabbath day and hallowed it

How many commandments are there, nine or ten? Many people object to this commandment. They want to qualify it and interpret it in such a way as to evacuate it of any force. It has no implications as far as their lives are concerned. I'm not merely talking about non-Christians. There are many Christians who have no regard for this commandment.

In both the Old Testament and the New Testament it is a point of controversy. It seems to have been more frequently broken than observed in the Old Testament. The Sabbath was often observed merely in outward form and not in the spiritual sense required. Many of the complaints of the Old Testament prophets centred on the cavalier and wicked attitude Israel often took to this commandment; in particular their neglect of it. This was one of the reasons why God sent the Children of Israel into exile in Babylon. God explained to Jeremiah that the land would enjoy the Sabbaths that they deprived it of over many centuries.

In the New Testament the Sabbath frequently became an occasion of controversy, notably with the Pharisees. It seems as if they followed Jesus around, especially on the Sabbath. They waited for Him to err. They listened intently to everything He said and carefully watched everything He did, with wicked intentions. They wanted to find something that they could construe as a violation of this commandment. On one occasion they criticised Christ when His disciples picked heads of grain in a field on the Sabbath. Mark records the incident:

> Now it happened that He went through the grainfields on the Sabbath; and as they went His disciples began to pluck the heads of grain. And the Pharisees said to Him, "Look, why do they do what is not lawful on the Sabbath?" But He said to them, "Have you never read what David did when he was in need and hungry, he and those with him: how he went into the house of God *in the days* of Abiathar the high priest, and ate the showbread, which is not lawful to eat except for the priests, and also gave some to those who were with him?" And He said to them, "The Sabbath was made for man, and not man for the Sabbath. Therefore the Son of Man is also Lord of the Sabbath" (Mark 2: 23-28).

They pounced on Jesus and His disciples and concluded that they were doing the same thing as the miller does when he grinds the corn in the mill to make flour. There were other occasions when the Pharisees objected to Christ's activity on the Sabbath. One of these occasions was when Jesus healed a man in the synagogue on the Sabbath. They were lurking in the shadows again ready to find fault. Another time the leader of the synagogue lectured Jesus about Sabbath observance saying there were six other days in which He could be active. It seems that Jesus went out of his way to provoke them.

But Jesus understood this commandment correctly. A cluster of beliefs, rules and traditions had grown around it which amounted to legalism. It had become a question of what can I do and what can't I do? The Pharisees formulated a whole list of things that were legitimate and other things that were not permitted. Their interpretation of this commandment was wrong. They missed the heart and purpose of it. They became very ingenious at working out how far you could go and what you could do and still keep this commandment. The phrase, 'a Sabbath day's journey', is used in the Bible. Luke uses it for example, '...they returned to Jerusalem from the mount called Olivet, which is near Jerusalem, a Sabbath day's journey' (Acts 1:12). This refers to the number of steps that were permitted on the Sabbath. The teachers of the law referred to the Pentateuch (books of the law), specifically Exodus and Numbers and fitted two verses together. They came up with the idea that two-thousand paces was the maximum permitted for a Sabbath day's journey. So the law was observed if you walked two-thousand paces but it was broken if you took an extra step. This distance is approximately three-quarters of a mile (1.2 kilometres). This was their typical way of thinking.

Inconvenient but Important

In the New Testament period Judaism had become legalistic. There was great religious and cultural diversity in the Greco-Roman world of that period. In other parts of the Roman Empire, outside Judea, paganism prevailed and there was no Sabbath concept so that the idea of abstaining from work for worship was unknown to Gentile nations. So Christians were being got at from both sides. The Jews trying to turn them into legalists and their Gentile friends and neighbours couldn't grasp the Sabbath concept and probably thought Sabbath observance was absurd.

For hundreds of years after Christ many Christians were at the bottom of society. They were slaves and servants. They were not part of the power structures. Imagine a slave coming to his master and saying, "It's Sunday and I don't work on Sundays". That would not have been tolerated by their masters. So Christians gathered together at very inconvenient hours in order that they might honour the Lord together on the first day of the week. Today in Muslim countries Friday is the Sabbath and Christians take advantage of the opportunity that affords to meet for fellowship.

They couldn't gather as we do at 11am (and 7pm). They had to work. They recognised the importance of keeping the Lord's Day and would come together early in the morning before dawn.

Pliny was the Governor of the Roman province of Bythinia in the middle of the land that we call Turkey today. Trajan was the Roman Emperor. Pliny was the sort of man who didn't like taking decisions for himself. He didn't want to offend those in higher positions of authority. He lacked initiative. So he wrote to Trajan and this correspondence is known as *The Rescript of Trajan*. In this document he is clearly concerned as to what he ought to do with Christians. He actually uses the word *Christian* to describe them. There was a type of Christian who didn't cause him any trouble. These were people who recanted their faith and denied the deity of Jesus. They would go along to the pagan temple and sacrifice to Caesar as God and repeat a certain form of words renouncing Jesus Christ. He had no problem with these people but he was concerned about another type of recalcitrant Christian who would not recant their faith in Jesus. His letter refers to the times when the Christians used to meet, 'At the beginning of the day, before dawn, they gather. They sing a hymn to Christ as God and they read of God'.

On one occasion Paul was on his way back to Jerusalem and came to a place called Troas where there were Christians. It is interesting to note that here were believers who met at the other end of the day. It was here that Paul on the first day of the week preached until midnight. A man named Eutychus was overwhelmed with sleep and fell from a third storey window. This shows the inconvenience they were willing to endure in order to meet together.

Thank God we are not in that situation. But doesn't it make it all the sadder that given the freedom we have that some are not so keen to observe the Lord's Day? Some Christians grumble about meeting together with God's people. They say the service is too long and we shouldn't have a morning service as well as an evening service and so on.

Sunday Sabbath

There are several passages of Scripture which indicate that believers met together on Sundays. Luke refers to the fact that Christians met on the first day of the week, 'Now on the first *day* of the week, when the disciples came together to break bread…' (Acts 20:7). In a New Testament passage that speaks about a financial collection for the saints, the apostle Paul says, 'On the first day of the week let each one of you lay something aside, storing up as he may prosper, that there be no collections when I come' (1 Corinthians 16:2).

The first day of the week was Sunday and this came to be known as the Lord's Day. Thus John says, 'I was in the Spirit on the Lord's Day...' (Revelation 1:10). After the resurrection of Christ the disciples were assembled together on a Sunday when Jesus appeared to them and spoke, particularly to the doubting Thomas. The Holy Spirit descended in power on Pentecost Sunday. It is clear that the New Testament church met on the first day of the week and that they had made the transition from Saturday to Sunday. It is obvious that it happened but not so obvious why it happened. Was it possibly proposed by somebody at a member's meeting? It was probably sanctioned by the apostolic leadership who authorised the change.

Changes in Society

Over the years there have been great changes in society. One change has been the introduction of Sunday trading. This, of course involves working on Sundays for many people. Attitudes regarding Sunday as a holy day have radically shifted. Cinemas are open, leisure centres, supermarkets and garden centres are all open for business on Sundays and have been for many years. The simplest thing to do is to have no distinctive view about the Sunday issue. And it appears this is the case for many Christians. The fourth commandment does not refer to Sunday anyway they say. It refers to the Jewish Sabbath and that is Saturday (actually sundown on Friday to sundown on Saturday).

Where in the New Testament do we find that this commandment has been transferred from the Saturday, the seventh day of the week, to Sunday, the first day of the week? We cannot produce a verse that simply says that. Despite difficulties of interpretation and application we must not throw the baby out with the bath-water. That is a calamitous thing to do and I fear that is what many Christians are doing. In reality many people who don't observe the Lord's Day don't observe the Sabbath principle on any other day of the week either. The Sabbath is a day of rest but it is also a day of reverence for God.

Principles

Despite the problems let us consider some of the principles in this commandment. First of all we should ask why it was that God gave it to us in the first place. There is something unusual about this commandment, something that it has in common with the next commandment ("honour your father and your mother…") but not with the others. We should note that both are expressed in positive terms. They are not negative restrictions expressed as "You shall not…" as all the others are. This commandment stands out. It is important to stress this because people who want to abolish the concept of Sunday observance say that it is a negative thing. But that is not the way it is presented in the Word of God. Scripture says it is to be remembered, not forgotten. It is to be kept holy.

The basic idea of holiness is separateness. The Hebrew word for holiness means 'distinct' or 'separate'. There is to be something distinctive and separate about the Sabbath day. It is not to be just like any other day. This commandment says that there are six days set aside for working, "Six days you shall labour and do all your work, but the seventh day *is* the Sabbath of the LORD your God. *In it* you shall do no work…" So, leaving aside the issue of Saturday versus Sunday the six days are allocated for work. This is a comprehensive statement and not just about one day. Many people when it comes to Sunday say, "There is so much undone, so much that needs doing that I must work today." But God gives instruction to work on the other six days. We are expected to desist from work on this one day.

If we look at how it is phrased we see that it is not only very comprehensive but it is also very kind:

> "Remember the Sabbath day, to keep it holy. Six days you shall labour and do all your work, but the seventh day *is* the Sabbath of the LORD your God. *In it* you shall do no work: you, nor your son, nor your daughter, nor your male servant, nor your female servant, nor your cattle, nor your stranger who *is* within your gates. For *in* six days the LORD made the heavens and the earth, the sea, and all that *is* in them, and rested the seventh day. Therefore the LORD blessed the Sabbath day and hallowed it."

This is not a commandment just for the aristocracy who live leisurely and indolent lives while their employees continue to toil and labour. Socially this was a very advanced concept and quite egalitarian for its time. Everybody, irrespective of class or status, was to have a rest. This was given so that people would not be exploited. They were entitled under the law to have a day off irrespective of what their masters thought about it. It was like a constitutional entitlement. Even the beasts of burden are taken care of in this commandment and this shows the kindness of God to all creatures.

Creation and Redemption

The Sabbath reminds us that God is our creator. God created the universe and every living thing in it in six days and rested on the seventh day, not because He was tired but He set a pattern; an example for us. God contemplated His work and we should take time to contemplate the creative and redemptive works of God on the Lord's Day.

It is interesting to look at the Deuteronomy version of the commandments. The Exodus version draws attention to what happened at the period of Exodus, " I *am* the LORD your God, who brought you out of the land of Egypt, out of the house of bondage" (Exodus 20:2). But Deuteronomy is a series of sermons that Moses preached and forty years on he restates the commandments. What is interesting about the variation in Deuteronomy 5 is that although the commandments are basically the same, there is more by way of exposition. Great emphasis is placed on God as their creator, redeemer and deliverer. This is important for us because we are to set aside time, once a week, to remember who made us and what He made us for. We are to remember His redemptive work and honour Him for the great deliverance He wrought for us on Calvary.

Christ's comment on the Sabbath is most interesting: "The Sabbath was made for man, and not man for the Sabbath..." (Mark 2:27). Here Jesus is saying people need the Sabbath. It was given out of the kindness of God for the benefit of all.

The Sabbath existed before the commandments were given to Moses on Mount Sinai. The very phraseology "Remember the Sabbath day, to keep it holy..." points to this (even though the word, 'remember' can be taken to mean, 'observe'). In Exodus the Sabbath is mentioned before the giving of the Decalogue:

> Then the LORD said to Moses, "Behold, I will rain bread from heaven for you. And the people shall go out and gather a certain quota every day, that I may test them, whether they will walk in My law or not. And it shall be on the sixth day that they shall prepare what they bring in, and it shall be twice as much as they gather daily."....And so it was, on the sixth day, *that* they gathered twice as much bread, two omers for each one. And all the rulers of the congregation came and told Moses. Then he said to them, "This *is w hat* the LORD has said: 'Tomorrow *is* a Sabbath rest, a holy Sabbath to the LORD. Bake what you will bake *to day*, and boil what you will boil; and lay up for yourselves all that remains, to be kept until morning.' "...Then Moses said, "Eat that today, for today *is* a Sabbath to the LORD; today you will not find it in the field. Six days you shall gather it, but on the seventh day, the Sabbath, there will be none."...For the LORD has given you the Sabbath; therefore He gives you on the sixth day bread for two days. Let every man remain in his place; let no man go out of his place on the seventh day." So the people rested on the seventh day (Exodus 16:4-5, 22-30).

It was explained more fully in the commandments but did not originate in them. We need to understand it in the light of all of God's revelation.

Market Day of the Soul

Before we ever come to the nitty-gritty of this commandment to find out what we can and can't do, we first need to ask the right questions. The basic question is not, what am I not permitted to do but rather what ought I to do? What does the Lord want me to do on this day? Why has God given it to us? What is the opportunity that it presents to us? What blessing does God have in mind in giving us this day?

The Puritans had a phrase to describe Sunday. They called it 'the market day of the soul'. When we think about that phrase it is worthy of note that market days occurred once a week. These were opportunities to get the things needful to sustain and nourish the body for the coming week. There you could buy bread, milk, fish, meat and vegetables. Whatever was needed could be obtained. It was a day when people had interaction with one another. Thus the market day of the soul is to be understood as the opportunity to come together in fellowship to get the things needed to nourish and sustain the soul. That is to pray, to worship and to listen to the Word of God read. It is an opportunity to be receptive to and responsive to the preached Word of God.

In truth many fail to observe this commandment and there is poor regard for observance of the Lord's Day. Where do we start to try to find how to apply this commandment in the ungodly age in which we live? We must begin by acknowledging that this is in fact one of the Ten Commandments. It is strange that many Christians accept that there is an eternal validity about the other nine but that this fourth commandment can be secondary, unimportant and nonessential. It is peculiar that people who profess to be guided and governed by the Word of God in all matters of faith and practice are willing to ignore this commandment because it is inconvenient. It is odd that it is seen as irrelevant by many today.

This commandment was given in a solemn way on Mount Sinai and it has not been rescinded. It is curious, therefore, that many Christians can so casually disregard it. It was written by the very finger of God. In Scripture it is presented to us as the direct speech of God. This should make us pause and consider what God is saying and not merely reject and dismiss this observance. It is considered by many to be queer and quaint and old fashioned to observe the Sabbath. It is seen as a bit fanatical (if one can be *a bit* fanatical). This is astonishing and perplexing.

The psalmist says, '*It is* good to give thanks to the LORD, and to sing praises to Your name, O Most High; to declare Your loving-kindness in the morning, and Your faithfulness every night' (Psalm 92:1-2). This ought to be a whole day in seven in which we are able to give ourselves to Him. It is not the Lord's half-day! It is the Lord's Day. It is not just a holiday, it is a holy day.

The Prevailing Culture

We live in a secular society that seems bent on overthrowing any legislation informed by Christian principles. Christians are perceived to be narrow-minded and old fashioned in a society which is multi-racial. The underlying principle has been that Christian values should not dominate in this multi-cultural context. But many people, including non-Christians, are beginning to say that the multi-cultural experiment is a failed project. There is a difference between being domineering and being dominant. Christian societies would do well to preserve their cultural identity and have the expectation that other immigrant cultures would fit in around their laws, customs and values.

This is not racist or fascist. Christians should not be domineering but the dominant Christian culture should be respected.

Sadly many Christians are influenced by the spirit of the age and so the Sabbath is seen as a day of rest and recreation and religious services are thought to be a burden. The attitude of many seems to be that we should get the religious bit over, give God His quota and then have the rest of the day free.

I like to walk with my wife by the river near our home. There are days when I feel tired and choose not to take that exercise. But I would be devastated if I was not able-bodied enough to do it. Are we sometimes like that about the Lord's Day? Do we take it for granted? Are we casual about observing it? If circumstances changed and it was made impossible or illegal how would we feel?

Many people see the Lord's Day in negative terms but this is quite wrong. It is not about what is forbidden it is about what is permitted and needful and nourishing for the soul. There are countries where Christians have to meet in secret because such fellowship is proscribed by law. It seems that these believers place a much higher value on the opportunity to worship God than some in our own society where there is liberty to meet whenever we want.

In Eastern Europe people who for many years could not meet openly for fellowship behind the Iron curtain of communism are now enjoying the opportunity to celebrate the Lord's Day publicly. They treasure it and honour it in well attended meetings. Today behind the bamboo curtains of many Asian countries Christian people are still repressed. In Western societies we don't have those restrictions and sadly we take such blessings for granted.

Getting it Right

This fourth commandment is part of the Decalogue and Scripture does not present it on a lower order to the other commandments. It is not put forward as something to be considered as a temporary requirement.

Sunday used to be special but it was also a day of doom and gloom. This is the problem of legalism; it marred the whole concept of the Sabbath in Christ's day and maybe in our history and experience it spoiled our appreciation of the Lord's Day. The Pharisees made Sabbath observance doable. In other words they qualified and quantified every detail of what was allowed and what was disallowed. As such, Sabbath observance became measurable. If you measured up you could say you kept the Sabbath and feel proud and pious. They externalised it. This is an attitude of mind that still exists today. There are people who observe the Sabbath in a superficial manner. Religious people are prone to it. So, even if we do observe the Lord's Day we should be careful not to become unduly proud of our piety. After all, let us remind ourselves, we are not justified by the keeping of the law. But the law is, nevertheless a standard to which we ought to aspire. It is something to aim for.

It has already been mentioned that one of the reasons for the Babylonian exile of God's people was that they ignored the complaints of the prophets and persistently and deliberately broke the second commandment concerning idols. But another reason was that they also misused and abused the Sabbath. God's patience was exhausted. They learned their lesson so that when they came back seventy years later they were never guilty (as a nation) of these two things again. As such they stood out as a unique phenomenon in the pagan Greco-Roman world.

We have noted how the religious leaders waited to pounce on Jesus about any perceived breach of the Sabbath. They were wrong in their attitudes but it must be noted that they placed great emphasis on Sabbath observance. They rightly understood that it was important but wrongly made it a burdensome religious duty.

Present Pressures

There are pressures on Christians today to work on Sundays. A person's job could be at risk if he or she refused work on Sunday. Many Christians have to work on Sundays of necessity. It is their duty in public service. People in emergency services such as ambulance drivers and paramedics, firemen, police officers, doctors and nurses and others have to work certain shifts that include Sundays.

With regard to sport it is not just the elite athletes who play matches on Sundays. Many sporting events at all levels are timetabled for Sundays. If boys or girls show an aptitude for sport they will be expected to be involved in training and competing on Sundays. The world emphasises the body over the soul. Both are important but the soul is more important than the body. We should look positively on Sunday and see it as an opportunity to be grasped. It is an opportunity to begin the week with God and we should guard the day and make it different. The profanity of the world pollutes. There is nothing edifying or glorifying in the world. There is much emphasis today on healthy living; eating the right foods, taking exercise and detoxifying the body. But Sunday is a day for detoxifying the soul. The Lord's Day can be an oasis where we can take spiritual refreshment and fortify ourselves for the week ahead.

Beware of swallowing the devil's arguments and regurgitating them. Because some people have to work on the Lord's Day does not mean that we have to concede the principle and join them. Hard cases make bad law. We should not abandon the Sabbath principle. Maybe you will have to work occasionally on Sunday but do so reluctantly and out of necessity, not out of choice (for extra money) and don't concede the principle in your heart.

We should not be deceived about arguments which say Sabbath observance is legalistic. Legalism is not the problem of this generation. The opposite is true. The Christian man who went to bed wearing his boots on Saturday night so that he would not have to exert himself by putting them on during the Sabbath was legalistic. But how many of us have that problem?

There are wonderful promises attached to keeping the Sabbath:

> "If you turn away your foot from the Sabbath, *from* doing your pleasure on My holy day, and call the Sabbath a delight, the holy *day* of the LORD honourable, and shall honour Him, not doing your own ways, nor finding your own pleasure, nor speaking *your own* words, Then you shall delight yourself in the LORD; and I will cause you to ride on the high hills of the earth, and feed you with the heritage of Jacob your father. The mouth of the LORD has spoken." (Isaiah 58:13-14).

Scripture exhorts us to observe the Sabbath as an example to others and it tells us that to fail to keep it is effectively tripping others up in their spiritual walk:

> There remains therefore a rest for the people of God. For he who has entered His rest has himself also ceased from his works as God *did* from His. Let us therefore be diligent to enter that rest, lest anyone fall according to the same example of disobedience (Hebrews 4:9-11).

But many people, including Christians tend to see this fourth commandment as unreasonable, antiquated and irrelevant. It is consequently neglected, rejected, reinterpreted or ignored.

Keeping Sunday Special

How seriously should we take it? At one time transgressions of this commandment incurred the death penalty. The penalty for breaking this commandment (death) was part of the judicial law of the Hebrew people of that time and is not part of the moral law of God. This means that the moral law to observe the Sabbath is still applicable but the penalty for breaking it is not. I doubt that anybody would advocate the reintroduction of this penalty. But surely it gives us insight into how serious a matter it is. The Lord's Day is not something to be anticipated with misery and foreboding rather it is something to be looked forward to. Normal duties during the rest of the week prevent us from giving God our undivided attention. Our occupational responsibilities inhibit us to a certain extent. So when it comes around in the cycle of the week we should squeeze out of it all the blessing we can get and we should give to God all that we can give.

The words of Christ should be borne in mind, '…Jesus answered him, saying, "It is written, 'Man shall not live by bread alone, but by every word of God' " (Luke 4:4, here Jesus is quoting from Deuteronomy). The soul needs sustenance. But we should not compartmentalize the soul and think that the Lord's Day is the only day for feeding it. We should take time to feed the soul every day but especially on Sunday. It is a very special day for us (at least it ought to be) but it is a very special day for the Lord. It is His day and we must give Him His due.

The eighth commandment (which we shall deal with later) says, "You shall not steal" and it applies to the Lord's Day. We should not steal that which should be devoted to God. This was the sin of Achan who hoarded booty for himself when he and the others in that army were told the spoils of victory in battle were to be devoted to God. The Lord's Day is not ours and we should be careful not to deprive Him of the honour due to Him on that day.

Some Christians seem to resent the Lord's Day as an intrusion. But let us remember that it is one of the commandments and they stand and fall together. May God give us the grace to revise our opinions and get rid of our prejudices and submit ourselves to the Word of God on this matter. Let us approach it positively, not with a sense of grudging acquiescence. It is not about what God is stopping us from doing. That is a wrong attitude and we need to repent of it. It is not a burden imposed by God and our attitude should not be that it is thankfully only one day in the week and it will soon be over. Rather we should plan for it. Gathering together for worship should be top of the list of our priorities. We should not be minimalist about it saying what is the least I can do to fulfil my obligation. Rather we should seek to maximise it and ask what is the most I can do to make this day special. The attitude of many seems to be, "what is the least I can do and still be a respectable Christian"? Though we may not articulate it in words, is that the attitude of our hearts? Children will catch the spirit from their parents and if Sunday is a chore and you just want to get the God bit out of the way then they will take on the same attitude.

How can we keep Sundays special? We can ensure we are not short of essentials, fuel for our cars food for our meals. We can try not to forget the milk or ice cream or whatever it is that would cause us to go to the shops on Sundays. We can get these things in on Saturday. We don't have to go shopping to supermarkets and garden centres on Sundays. If you are an employer don't burden your staff so that you can free yourself up on Sunday because this is not in keeping with the spirit or letter of the fourth commandment. The Sunday dinner shouldn't be such a chore that it absorbs much of your time and energy. Men shouldn't sit down at home and allow their wives to wait on them hand and foot so that they can have a Sabbath rest. Rather let the men help and ease the burden so that their wives can have a Sabbath rest too.

Consider that there are better things to do with your time on the Lord's Day. We can read good Christian books. We can read the

Scriptures and meditate on them. There is very little space for silence and meditation in our world but in the Lord's Day we can set aside time for this. If there is a part of the Bible you don't understand you could study it. We can engage in intercessory prayer. Sunday is a good time to prepare for the mid week Bible study. Students should try to study on the other six days of the week. Try to plan your work so as to avoid doing it on the Lord's Day. Your mind will benefit from the rest. It may be difficult to be consistent but it is important to have the right aim and to approach this positively.

What would Jesus do? Scripture records what He did on the Sabbath? He exercised mercy in healing the sick. He met with His disciples. Will we be with other believers on the Lord's Day when Jesus is present in resurrection power? When we meet with Him He removes our doubts and strengthens our faith. Will we rest from work? Will we worship? Will we be concerned with deeds of mercy? We must not be under the influence of the spirit of the age which is essentially atheistic and hedonistic. There is nothing wrong with liking pleasure but our pleasure as believers should include loving God and the company of His people. Let us ask what is right? What does God want me to do? Let us prayerfully consider the issues raised by the practical application of this commandment. Let us seek to find God's heart and follow that way. We must go through this process alone with God and live with integrity in accordance with the teaching of Scripture and in harmony with a spiritually informed conscience. The question, 'what does God require of us', must matter to us.

God gives us a glorious opportunity for the edification of the saints and the evangelisation of sinners. We can help others and exalt Him and we can do all this on the Lord's Day. It is a day of rest that anticipates the eternal rest that will one day be ours in heaven. Let us look to Him and be taken up with the things of God.

The Fifth Commandment

Honour your father and your mother,
that your days may be long upon the land
which the Lord your God is giving you

It may seem a little strange that God should find it necessary to issue such a commandment. One might expect that children would naturally honour their parents. What does it mean to "honour you father and your mother"? It means to respect them, love them and obey them. God establishes a moral standard in the Decalogue which is beneficial to society as a whole. Here, in this particular commandment, He institutes a structure of authority at a family level. The apostle Paul, in his letter to the Ephesians, spoke about the relationship between children and parents:

> Children, obey your parents in the Lord, for this is right. ***"Honour your father and mother,"*** which is the first commandment with promise: ***"that it may be well with you and you may live long on the earth"*** (Ephesians 6:1-3).

Paul quoted the fifth commandment but adds a qualifying comment which is implied but not overtly stated in the commandment itself. He says, 'obey your parents ***in the Lord***' (emphasis added). This means that it is right and good to obey one's parents inasmuch as their counsel and commands are godly and wise. One would not be expected to obey a parent's instructions to do something which is morally wrong and clearly forbidden in the other commandments. We proceed with this proviso in mind.

In Mark 12 we encounter Christ fielding questions from various groups of people. The Pharisees ask if it lawful to pay taxes to Caesar. The Sadducees ask about the resurrection and the Scribes ask which of the commandments is the greatest. These were establishment figures and determined enemies of Christ. Frequently these people did not ask questions with the purpose of genuinely seeking answers. Often they were trying not only to test Christ but to trap Him. They hoped He would make a mistake and they were ready to pounce and punish any error. But it is fascinating to see how Jesus handled them on different occasions. In reply to the Scribe's question (which may have been sincere[1]) Jesus summarised the Ten Commandments.

> Jesus answered him, "The first of all the commandments *is: Hear, O Israel, the LORD our God, the LORD is one. And you shall love the LORD your God with all your heart, with all your soul, with all your mind, and with all your strength.* This *is* the first commandment. And the second, like *it, is* this: *You shall love your neighbour as yourself.* There is no other commandment greater than these" (Mark 12:29-31).

Jesus does not actually quote the commandments in his answer. Christ is saying that the commandments are about our relationship with God and also about our human relationships.

*

---

[1] Nevertheless a few verses later (38-40) Jesus told people to beware of the Scribes and He condemns them for their pomp and ceremony, their long-winded prayers and their sense of self-importance. Jesus identifies them as hypocrites and points out that their privileged position in public is undeserved because in private they are unmerciful to the most vulnerable in society.

There is a division between the first four commandments and the other six. Many today would see the first four as irrelevant but view the other six as good for society. Many today would talk about morality without religion. They would regard the first four commandments as an unnecessary encumbrance. The humanist thinks these four commandments are religious rubbish. The first four commandments tell us who God is and how He is to be worshipped. They speak of the honour of God's name and Sabbath observance. But many people in society discount the contemporary relevance of these. They say it might have suited society in a previous generation but it is meaningless today. But there is sufficient correlation between the decline in religion and the decline in morality to warrant the view that the decline in religion has been detrimental to the health of the society.[2] History has rolled on a bit and given its verdict. Abortion has increased; crime is more common, society has become more violent and marriage breakdown is widespread. It is a wonder how those who confidently broadcast humanist and secularist theories a generation ago cannot see where such a philosophy has taken society.

Morality without religion doesn't work. That's why God begins the commandments with Himself: who He is, how He is to be honoured and how His day is to be respected. Because God knows that we cannot ultimately have morals without a true and genuine religion (i.e. faith in God).[3] The social commandments are:

5. "Honour your father and your mother, that your days may be long upon the land which the LORD your God is giving you."

---

[2] Taking a standard from the British Isles in the 1950s

[3] That is not to say that all atheists, agnostics and humanists are amoral or immoral. It has to be acknowledged (and not begrudgingly) that many people who are not religious live decent, law-abiding lives. It is also necessary to be honest here and say that some religious people do not live decent, law-abiding lives.

6. "You shall not murder."

7. "You shall not commit adultery."

8. "You shall not steal."

9. "You shall not bear false witness against your neighbour."

10. "You shall not covet your neighbour's house; you shall not covet your neighbour's wife, nor his male servant, nor his female servant, nor his ox, nor his donkey, nor anything that *is* your neighbour's."

Most people would not quibble with the sense of these rules. Most people would agree that if they were observed society would be better. But if we were given this list and asked to order them in priority, which of us would put the fifth commandment at the top? Some of us will remember their order but if we were to set that aside and sort them in terms of what we would consider the most important of these six commandments to be, I think many of us would jump immediately to the sixth commandment, "you shall not murder". How many of us would prioritise the fifth commandment, "honour your father and your mother"? We would tend to think that the prohibition on murder should take precedence in the list. I'm sure we would say that to dishonour our parents is wrong but it is not as grave as murder.

But in the Old Testament those who dishonoured their parents could be put to death by stoning. Clearly it was a very serious matter. This action was intended to purge an evil from within the community and to act as a deterrent and thereby maintain a disciplined and regulated social order (Leviticus 20:9; Deuteronomy 21:18).

Right Order

Maybe we would give some of the other commandments precedence over the fifth but God does not put it like that. And whatever God does is never done in some kind of random or haphazard way. There is always something deliberate, measured and ordered in the steps of God. He puts this commandment at the head of this list of the second group of regulations. Undoubtedly God knew what He was doing and He did it deliberately, for a purpose.

Why? The psalmist says that, 'God sets the solitary in families' (Psalm 68:6). We belong to families. In Genesis we read of the original family, Adam and Eve and their children, Cain and Abel and Seth. The family is the building block of society. If there is corruption in the family then it will spread to society. Much of the social unrest in society right now is centred on children (teenagers and younger) involved in anti-social behaviour. Cities are scourged with gangs of young people presenting an intimidating and dangerous presence in communities. Gun crime and knife crime among the young is all too familiar. People's efforts to reclaim the streets seem to be ineffective. Anti-Social Behaviour Orders (A.S.B.O.s) are not producing the desired results. Many young people tend to see these as a badge of honour or a trophy to be proud of. Parental control orders are generally useless in the way they are currently operated. The social and economic factors which create a climate where young people turn to crime need to be addressed. Many schools and parents do take responsibility for the discipline of young people but many parents do not. These problems can ultimately be traced back to families where there is discord and strife and flagrant repudiation of this commandment.

If the first four commandments are not respected by parents they will be bereft of spiritual integrity. Their counsel and commands are ad hoc or inconsistent and lacking in moral coherence. They are essentially impoverished because they live according to their own individual and impaired standards and there is no consensus about what is right and wrong. The cost, to society, of dispensing with

God, was not immediately obvious but it has become increasingly noticeable over the last several decades.

Respect for Older People

Many people regard this commandment as nonsense because we live in a culture in Western society that has little or no respect for older people. We have had to enact laws to ensure that age discrimination is not practiced in employment. This is a good thing but it points to the fact that such safeguards are required because age discrimination is a reality. Older people are generally thought to be past their *best before* or *sell by* date. The common perception among younger people is that older people don't understand them because they are not on the same wave-length. They believe younger people understand the world better.

Increasingly young people go to one another for advice rather than go to older people. They see older people as irrelevant because they come from an older generation and give advice that might have worked a generation ago but can have no contemporary value.

There is a tragic example of that in the Old Testament. Solomon died and was succeeded by his son Rehaboam. The people came to him and asked him to back off because his father had ruled with a rod of iron. He took counsel. He went to his old counsellors and they advised him go along with it. They said that his authority would not be diminished at all and that he would have them eating out of the palm of his hand. They said this would be a good start to his reign. They had seen the bitterness and resentment spreading through the nation because of the hardness of the rule and so they counselled wisely.

But Rehaboam then called in his young friends and put the same matter to them. He explained how he had been petitioned to back off from the stand his father had taken and asked for their advice.

These younger men gave contrary and unwise advice. They told Rehaboam not to go along with this request. They said that if he gives in on this point that the people will walk all over him. They tell him to show them who is boss. They tell him to show them that he is king and that he is in charge of the nation. And in 1 Kings 12 we have the sad story given to us and this is what he said:

> Then the king answered the people roughly, and rejected the advice which the elders had given him; and he spoke to them according to the advice of the young men, saying, "My father made your yoke heavy, but I will add to your yoke; my father chastised you with whips, but I will chastise you with scourges!" (13-14).

We cannot say that all older people by virtue of their age alone are wise. There are silly fogies too. Age does not necessarily bring wisdom. Some older people live in a time warp and they romanticise the past and perpetuate the myth of nostalgia. They like to reminisce and many people tend to avoid them because they consider them to be doddery old bores. Some young people are exceptionally wise but in general terms age and experience should bring wisdom.

In the current debate about gun crime and knife crime amongst young people in Britain there is an evident lack of consensus as to how this problem should be tackled. Some people are calling for tougher laws and stricter enforcement while others are saying that is just a middle-class approach to a problem and it is preferable that the young people themselves be consulted. Those who make this kind of argument say we must listen to the young people involved in this illicit activity if we are to find a solution or at least devise appropriate and effective tactics to combat the problem. It is an approach favoured by many.

Others would argue that it is unwise to ask illegally armed and dangerously violent juvenile delinquents, who engage in violence as a recreational activity, to solve the problem. This latter group would contend that many of these young people are bored, idle, stoned, ignorant, uneducated, illiterate, inarticulate, socially inept and maladjusted and that decent citizens should not involve them in a consultation process.

In reality these estranged and disillusioned youth stab and shoot people because they don't like the colour of somebody's skin or because somebody has unwittingly strayed into their stomping ground. They kill for money, for fun or because some unfortunate accidentally bumped into them. These people seriously dishonour their parents and as a result many are dying in the streets and forfeiting the longevity promised in the fifth commandment, "…that your days may be long…" Yet they are lost souls and have the potential to be full participants in society and contribute constructively if only they could be salvaged from destructive environments and harmful relationships. As Christians we should be trying to reach these boys and girls with the gospel, because it is only the transforming power of God that can make a real and lasting difference.

The lack of consensus in how to best tackle this issue contributes to the problem. Intervention strategies are needed but crime must be punished and that punishment should also have a rehabilitative dimension.

A Spiritual Dimension to a Social Problem

There is a spiritual dimension to this social problem. The family has been in the front line of Satan's attacks since Adam and Eve transgressed in the Garden of Eden (Genesis 3). At that stage they were just husband and wife without children. After they ate the forbidden fruit Adam was interrogated by God and what did he do? He blamed his wife. Then in the fourth chapter we read about the first murder. How Adam and Eve must have regretted the day they disobeyed God and got themselves into this terrible state of affairs.

The devil had got into the very heart of the family and he is still doing it. There is abundant evidence of this in society today where the concept of the traditional family is old fashioned. Behind all this is the strategy of Satan.

The fifth commandment is about respecting elders, most immediately in the family and showing them honour as parents. Proverbs is a book full of instruction. The basic perspective of the book is that somebody who is older and wiser is speaking to somebody who is younger, more naïve and not as experienced. In the opening chapter we read, 'My son, hear the instruction of your father, and do not forsake the law of your mother; for they *will be* a graceful ornament on your head, and chains about your neck' (1:8-9; see also 4:1 and 6:20). In a normal and healthy relationship between parents and children this is how things ought to be. Giving honour to parents is something that adorns and beautifies.

Scripture tells us that Jesus was subject to his parents and that He obeyed them. They would have told Him what to do and He would have followed their instructions. Parents have a great responsibility. Do we honour our parents? Do we love them? Do we respect them? Do we obey them? As parents, are we worthy of that love and respect? Do we set the right example? Or is it a case of, "do what I say but don't be what I am"? As young people do we have a spirit of rebelliousness in us? The fifth commandment has never been revoked. It still has all the authority and force it had when God first gave it. The punishment for failing to observe it has passed away with the judicial aspect of the law but the commandment itself is part of the universal and abiding law of God and is still applicable today. It is part of the fabric of authority in society and when it begins to unravel society is stripped of its garments and is naked and ought to be ashamed.

first gave it. The punishment for failing to observe it has passed away with the judicial aspect of the law but the commandment itself is part of the universal and abiding law of God and is still applicable today. It is part of the fabric of authority in society and when it begins to unravel society is stripped of its garments and is naked and ought to be ashamed.

The Old Problem of the Young

The commandments are about four-thousand years old. They tell us that many of the moral problems of today are not new. Secular literature also bears testimony to this. The philosopher, Aristotle (384 B.C.-322 B.C.) once said:

> Our youth now live in luxury. They have bad manners and contempt for authority. They show disrespect for their elders and love to chatter in place of exercise. Children are now tyrants, not the servants of their households. They no longer rise when their parents enter the room. They contradict their parents, chatter in front of company, gobble their food and tyrannise their teachers.[4]

This sounds strangely modern in some ways. It may be an ancient problem but it is nevertheless sad to see the widespread disregard of the fifth commandment in our day.

Parents

There are two aspects of teaching in this commandment, one affecting the parent and the other the child. The apostle Paul wrote, giving Timothy pastoral instruction and among many other things he stated: '...that in the last days...men will be lovers of themselves, lovers of money, boasters, proud, blasphemers, disobedient to parents, unthankful, unholy, unloving, unforgiving, slanderers, without self-

---

[4] *Youth Bible*, 1983, Nashville: Tennessee, Nelson World, New Century Version (anglicised edition) p.1186 (note on Romans chapter 2).

control, brutal, despisers of good' (2 Timothy 3:1-3). In this list of sins and misconduct, disrespect for parental wisdom and authority is included as an indicator of a pervasive disorder and malady in society.

There is no doubt that parents must bear much of the blame for the trouble with young people today. The Word of God places great emphasis upon headship. This is a divine principle. Those in positions of authority at home, in school, in business, in the nation or the church are held responsible by God for guidance and discipline. All too often delinquency in young people can be traced back to delinquent parents. The word 'delinquent' means 'to neglect' or 'fail in duty'. Scripture clearly states that husbands and wives are to love one another, and stay together as long as they live (Ephesians 5:28-33 and Romans 7:2, 3). However, many marriages break down. Families are broken up and new partnerships are formed often with devastating effect upon the offspring of the original union. Psalm 127 says, 'children *are* a heritage from the LORD' (v.3). But do parents view their children in this way today? It is inevitable that in circumstances such as these, children are uncertain who their true parents are. For in many instances they spend time with both parents and step-parents, mixing with children from different unions. Those who are acquainted with agriculture know that it is most difficult to put a lamb to a ewe which is not its mother. Neither will settle and frequently the ewe will reject it because it is not hers.

What has this to do with the fifth commandment? It has everything to do with it. There are two aspects of truth incorporated in this commandment; one concerns the parent and the other the child. This commandment commences, "honour your father and your mother." The word 'honour' implies obedience, but it means very much more. Indeed it is a comprehensive word conveying the thought and sensitive and wise pastoral care is needed instead of judgemental attitudes. But the commandments must be respected.

There is profound and ancient wisdom in the commandments but it is not human wisdom; it is divine revelation. The psalmist says, 'I have seen the consummation of all perfection, *But* Your commandment *is* exceedingly broad' (Psalm 119:96). The Word of God is an incomparable treasure which is greatly undervalued. The commandments cover every aspect of life; many issues enter into them. From other Scriptures we soon discover the depth of teaching contained in the fifth commandment. Parents have great responsibility to their children. They are to, 'bring them up in the training and admonition of the Lord' (Ephesians 6:4). It is incumbent upon parents to endeavour to make God's ways and Word known to their children. Timothy's mother instructed him in the Scriptures from early childhood: 'from childhood you have known the Holy Scriptures, which are able to make you wise for salvation through faith which is in Christ Jesus (2 Timothy 3:15). One of the most important words in Scripture to parents is found in the book of Proverbs, 'Train up a child in the way he should go, and when he is old he will not depart from it' (22:6). This verse speaks of parental authority regarding general training, and covers the secular as well as the spiritual.

Parents are to be kind and loving, but not over over-indulgent, as invariably a spoilt or untrained child will bring embarrassment upon a parent rather than honour. David spoiled his son Adonijah: 'his father had not rebuked him at any time by saying, "Why have you done so?" ' (1 Kings 1:6). David did not correct him, and this son in later years became a great grief to his father. When divine principles are ignored, there are inevitable bad consequences.

If parents are to retain honour amongst their children then they must maintain authority. Solomon tells us, He who spares his rod hates his son, but he who loves him disciplines him promptly (Proverbs 13:24). Again some chapters later in the same book we read: 'Do not withhold correction from a child, for *if* you beat him with a rod, he will not die. You shall beat him with a rod, and deliver his soul from hell' (Proverbs 23:13-14). To the contemporary mind this sounds terrible. It seems as if Christians are actively promoting child abuse. But this is not what is advocated in Scripture. It is wrong to act in a rage or in a fit of temper. Self-control is a fruit of the Holy Spirit. Discipline must be administered fairly and proportionately and above all in love.

That sounds like a contradiction to many people. They say how can you love and beat your child? But Scripture says that if we fail to discipline our children then we fail to love them properly. Paul's letters to the Colossians and Ephesians tell fathers not to provoke their children to anger because this will discourage them (Ephesians 6:4; Colossians 3:21). This is a most important exhortation. Parents must be prudent in disciplining a child and must always be disciplined themselves.

Saul spoke to his son Jonathan in a rage, 'Then Saul's anger was aroused against Jonathan, and he said to him, "You son of a perverse, rebellious *w o m a n!*" (1 Samuel 20:30). That was far from a wise manner of correction. In fact Saul is a glaring example in Scripture of the way parents are not to discipline their children. He would strike without cause, which a parent must never do. Once he threw a javelin at his son whilst they were having a meal, with the result that Jonathan arose from the table and left in fierce anger (1 Samuel 20:33-34). He treated his son shamefully and what parent has a right to expect honour if they act like this? Parents must never be tyrants.

Partiality and favouritism towards a member of the family is also reprehensible. Jacob favoured Joseph and the result was other members of the family failed to honour Jacob. This is evident in the action they took against Joseph, which was heart-breaking for their father.

Children must never be asked by their parents to do that which is inherently wrong. Saul commanded Jonathan to fetch David saying, 'He shall surely die' Jonathan refused and in doing so did not honour his father's instructions but he was not wrong in refusing to obey such a wicked command (1 Samuel 20:30-42). Inconsistent parents who act in an irresponsible and irrational manner do not deserve honour as their life discourages the child from obedience. It must always be remembered that just as children are required to honour their parents, parents must remember not to dishonour their children.

The example that parents give and the love they show are essential elements in training a child. Children will despise their parents if father and mother do not live up to that which they profess to believe. How can a child come to a right understanding of morals if parents find entertainment in obscene jokes and immoral activities? How can a child be trained in the evils of alcohol if parents overindulge in it? Many parents today have seen their children's marriage flounder, yet have been unable to help or counsel because they themselves have been divorced.[5] If parents are to be honoured by their children, then their example must be right. Love is the overriding element in the training of children and it should permeate rebuke, correction and punishment.

No child can be loved too much. To spoil or indulge a child's every whim is not love. But to demonstrate true affection engenders confidence, security and a sense of belonging to which a child will respond. In the spiritual realm it is said of God's children, 'We love

---

[5] It is important to acknowledge here that there may be an innocent party to a divorce.

Him because He first loved us' (1 John 4:19). These words set out a principle which is also applicable within the human family. Children love their parents because their parents first loved them. But if parents are cold and formal in their relationship with their families showing no real affection then they must not be disappointed or upset if they receive little in return. Love begets love. If children are conscious from their earliest days of warm, ardent love it has the effect of enveloping them so that throughout their lives it will make them feel secure. Where it is absent it causes them to feel insecure. The place of love in the home cannot be over-stressed and it certainly has a great bearing on the fifth commandment. We need to pray for our children that they may be kept from the appalling evil of this age and that they come to salvation in Christ.

Children

Having dealt at length with the responsibilities of parents we now look at what God requires from children. The commandment states, "Honour your father and your mother". We have already stated that this means that children are to respect their parents. It does not matter whether the child is seven or seventy years old, that respect for parents is due to them. The writer to the Hebrews says, 'we have had human fathers who corrected *us*, and we paid *them* respect' (Hebrews 12:9). In a healthy parent/child relationship where parents walk circumspectly before their children, this will usually be the case. There will be an inbuilt respect mingled with affection. Children should not to be afraid of their parents. The honour talked about in this commandment is a veneration begotten by confidence in, and love toward the parent.

This will be manifest in the way the children treat their parents. Children respond to the example shown by their parents. Scripture states of a mother that: 'Her children rise up and call her blessed' (Proverbs 31:28). Children of all age groups are instructed in the

Word of God to honour their parents. Joseph was a mighty prince in Egypt but when his aged father came down to Egypt after a long separation Joseph treated him with great respect and affection. When they met Joseph, 'fell on his neck and wept on his neck a good while' (Genesis 46:29). Such incidents are not recorded in Scripture just to make interesting reading. They are inspired by the Holy Spirit for our instruction and here it can be seen that Joseph, a grown man and a man of important status, revered his father.

To children and younger people who are still under parental control, God says in His Word, 'My son, hear the instruction of your father, and do not forsake the law of your mother' (Proverbs 1:8). This is all embracing; it most certainly includes spiritual instruction. But it is not confined to that alone, for wise parents will give guidance on all matters, to which children should give heed. When Isaac called Jacob and blessed him he instructed: "You shall not take a wife from the daughters of Canaan" (Genesis 28:1). Every Christian parent should ensure that their children who are believers, are instructed in the Scriptural teaching that they are not to become unequally yoked with an unbeliever (2 Corinthians 6:14) and it is the duty of the child to honour this instruction.

It is recorded that Eli's sons did not heed their father (1 Samuel 2:25). They were disobedient to him and they were described as corrupt and Scripture says they did not know the Lord (1 Samuel 2:12). When children rebel against sound biblical instruction it invariably results in sorrow or tragedy. When a child has been disobedient, then it is essential that there is consistency in punishment and in discipline. Idle threats are worse than useless. It is disastrous when a father punishes the child, and then the mother gives sympathy. This ruins children and destroys marriages. Parents must be united in bringing up their children, chastening them in love, which should cause the children to be sincerely sorry for their actions. In this they honour their father and mother. Young people must remember that a failure to honour parents is a failure to honour God. It is a breaking of His Law which says, "Honour your father and your mother"

We have already noted the promise attending adherence to this commandment which is emphasised more in the New Testament:

> Children, obey your parents in the Lord, for this is right. *"Honour your father and mother,"* which is the first commandment with promise. *"that it may be well with you and you may live long on the earth"* (Ephesians 6:1-3).

For young people to know the blessing of God upon their lives they must obey God by honouring their parents. No parents are perfect so children should remember that they are obeying God in honouring and obeying their parents and this will help them to do so with grace. This commandment, in its dual aspect, is as relevant today as it was when it was first given.

The Sixth Commandment

You shall not murder

od wants people to respect the sanctity of life and so this commandment was given to prohibit murder. Some versions of the Bible say, "you shall not kill" but *murder* conveys the true meaning better than *kill*. This commandment is not a ban on all killing but it does, clearly, disallow homicide. People were allowed to kill animals for food and for sacrifice and the death penalty was not merely commended by God; it was commanded. Thus we read in Exodus:

> "He who strikes a man so that he dies shall surely be put to death. However, if he did not lie in wait, but God delivered *him* into his hand, then I will appoint for you a place where he may flee. But if a man acts with premeditation against his neighbour, to kill him by treachery, you shall take him from My altar, that he may die" (21:12-14).

The taking of a person's life is a very serious matter. These verses in Exodus reveal that different punishments were administered to those who took a human life and this depended on the circumstances. Violent action which resulted in a person's death was deemed to be different to premeditated murder and this was reflected in the respective penalties imposed.

Some people feel that they have never broken any of the commandments but they are seriously deluded souls. But most people feel that there are a few commandments they have not broken and this one concerning murder is one of that number. It is quite sobering, therefore, to consider the words of Jesus on this matter:

> "Do not think that I came to destroy the Law or the Prophets. I did not come to destroy but to fulfil. For assuredly, I say to you, till heaven and earth pass away, one jot or one tittle will by no means pass from the law till all is fulfilled…For I say to you, that unless your righteousness exceeds *the righteousness* of the scribes and Pharisees, you will by no means enter the kingdom of heaven. You have heard that it was said to those of old, *You shall not murder,* and whoever murders will be in danger of the judgment. But I say to you that whoever is angry with his brother without a cause shall be in danger of the judgment" (Matthew 5:17-22).

I think we would agree that our observance of the law hardly matches, let alone succeeds, that of the Pharisees. Jesus is saying here that it is futile to depend on our own righteousness as a means of gaining access to the kingdom of heaven. He is saying that even the Pharisees determined and detailed adherence to the law was not sufficient grounds to warrant entry to the kingdom of heaven. This must have rocked the listening Scribes and Pharisees back on their heels. They prided themselves on keeping the commandments and saw themselves as innocent of violating them.

But nobody is innocent of violating the commandments. Jesus referred to the sixth commandment, "You shall not murder" but points out that to harbour hatred or anger in your heart is where murder begins. In this sense many who feel they are innocent of murder are in fact guilty before the law and will face judgement. The law is a standard which must be observed inasmuch as possible but it cannot save. Only Christ can save and the law drives us to God for mercy and grace.

What are the commandments? Are they outward technical rules to be ticked off? Or do they express spiritual principles? Surely the commandments are not just about our actions but also about our attitudes. This principle runs right throughout the Sermon on the Mount. Jesus mentions *anger* as a violation of this commandment which would incur judgement. Anger in some circumstances is proper. Jesus was angry when He drove traders out of the temple courts. In one parable He calls a man a 'fool'. But Christ's anger was a righteous indignation without sin. Paul said to the Ephesians, "'Be angry, and do not sin": do not let the sun go down on your wrath' (Ephesians 4:26).[1]

Jesus demolished the interpretation which the Scribes and Pharisees put on the sixth commandment. He extended it in a most uncomfortable way as far as all of us are concerned. God says, "You shall not murder". Why? This brings us to the question; what is man? Many people in the world: cultured, educated people don't know what a human being is. Many say we are related to animals and that we have evolved from a lower species of animal. These people are not fully (spiritually) aware of what it is to be human. As we examine this commandment we have to ask this question first; what is man? What is it that is distinctive about us?

The answer is that we have been made in the image of God. We have souls.

> Then God said, "Let Us make man in Our image, according to Our likeness; let them have dominion over the fish of the sea, over the birds of the air, and over the cattle, over all the earth and over every creeping thing that creeps on the earth." So God created man in His *o w n* image; in the image of God He created him; male and female He created them. Then God blessed them, and God said to them, "Be fruitful and multiply; fill the earth and subdue

---

[1] "Be angry, and do not sin" is a quotation from Psalm 4:4.

it; have dominion over the fish of the sea, over the birds of the air, and over every living thing that moves on the earth" (Genesis 1:26-28).

This is not written of any of the other animals that God brought into existence. This is the distinctive feature of mankind. That was said before the fall of man recorded in Genesis 3. When we come to the other side of the Fall and the Flood we see God entering into covenant with man and laying down certain stipulations, "Whoever sheds man's blood, by man his blood shall be shed; for in the image of God He made man" (Genesis 9:6). Here we are given the reason why we are not to murder. When a person murders somebody they strike at the very image of God. Some animal rights activists will put human life at risk to protect animals but this is unbiblical, however legitimate they think their cause may be. All life belongs to God and is important to God but humanity is God's special creation. He is the giver of life and He has the right to take it. That prerogative belongs to Him.

There is some confusion and misunderstanding about this commandment. There are some people who say that it forbids the taking of any life, animal or human and so they practice vegetarianism or adopt a vegan position. People are free to be vegetarians if they wish but it is not wrong to eat animals. This is not condemned in Scripture. Whatever the reason for vegetarianism may be it has no biblical warrant. Meat eating is normal in Scripture. One may have certain sensibilities about meat eating and one may adopt a sentimental diet to accommodate their way of thinking but it is wrong to seek to justify such a position as a biblical view.

This commandment reinforces the distinctiveness of mankind and the value of human life. We seem to be obsessed with murder and this is reflected in the fact that it is a major theme in many films, such as psychological thrillers, true crime stories, detective programmes and T.V. series. It is a moot point as to whether this desensitises us to the notion of homicide. But in reality murder is prohibited because it is abhorrent to God. We live in a wicked world where murder is all too common. This commandment speaks to us on issues such as: abortion, euthanasia, mercy killing and suicide. What about the death penalty or war? Are there any circumstances where we are permitted to kill fellow human beings? Does this commandment rule out all wars or are there just wars? We have to go to the Bible for the answers.

God made it clear that the tribes and nations that inhabited the Promised Land were to be wiped out. This genocide and ethnic cleansing was authorised by God and is one of the most difficult issues of the Old Testament to understand. It is disturbing to read of such incidents in Scripture. Our hearts are frequently moved to pity the peoples who were exterminated in these accounts. We wonder how God could condone, commend and command such action. But it should be borne in mind that many of these peoples indulged in extremely evil practices and the only way of eradicating these was to stamp out the culture in which they thrived.

We might even question His benevolence. How are we to understand such things? Here we fall back on our faith and trust that He is omnipotent, omniscient and benevolent. Who are we to question God? His ways are not our ways (Isaiah 55:8-9). He is infinitely wise and we cannot expect to comprehend all His doings. We cannot be so arrogant as to assume we know better. We should not be so deluded that we think we are more compassionate than Him. How dare we suggest that He is malevolent! We need to have enough humility to accept that there are things we do not and cannot understand. We need to have enough faith to believe that His ways are good and best. We ought to have enough personal experience of Him to realise that His integrity is beyond question or doubt.

Most violence, including wars come from the wrong attitudes of people's hearts. Ungodly attitudes and actions are at the core of civil and international wars. Greed is the reason for most conflicts. The lust for power has caused many wars in history. But the alternative; pacifism, is not a biblical position. Christianity is not pacifist. There may be a necessity for war to prevent greater evil.

But war is a terrible thing. The Christian church has a responsibility and opportunity to offer a radically different alternative to the current trigger-happy approach to solving conflict in our world. We are not promoting absolute pacifism as the ideal Christian position because there is no Scriptural warrant for such a stance. Sadly there have been times in history (and there will likely be such times again) when war becomes necessary. There are evil despots who brutalise and terrorise their own people and abuse their power by invading neighbouring countries. There are regimes that harbour hatred against other countries and seek to accumulate weapons of mass destruction with the intention to annihilate others. There are powers that would engage in 'ethnic cleansing' and policies of genocide.

Nevertheless war must always be the last and least favoured option. War should never be declared unless and until every other avenue has been thoroughly explored and exhausted. War should be defensive rather than offensive. Even then those who declare a 'just war' should do so with the purest motives, the greatest reluctance and the heaviest of hearts. Because the human cost (military and civilian) in terms of the suffering that will inevitably result from war is so truly awful, the ultimate objective of war must, ironically, be sustainable peace itself. War must always be the last resort, in a cause that is just, where the intention is noble and likely to succeed in its goals.

The means must be proportionate and non-combatants should be guaranteed immunity. The rules of the Geneva Convention on

Human Rights governing the rules of engagement in times of war must be upheld and no nation on earth should be exempt from accountability for war crimes. Admittedly the post Cold-War world where Islamic fundamentalism issues *fatw a* and declares *jihad* needs to be factored in to an appropriate Christian response.

Christians ought to be a people who are essentially committed to non-violence. We are to offer the other cheek to those who would strike us so that peace may prevail.

Jesus calls the Christian not only to non-violence but also to proactive peacemaking. Christ demands that His disciples love their enemies and do good to those who hate them. Furthermore we are to pray for those who persecute us. Jesus practised what He preached. He was gentle to the point of not resisting betrayal, arrest, trial, sentence, flogging, mocking and execution. He did not retaliate: 'He was led as a lamb to the slaughter' (Isaiah 53:7). In His agony Christ prayed for those who nailed Him to the cross, 'Father, forgive them'. This is the way of the cross and Christ invites us to follow Him by taking up our cross daily. The teaching and example of Jesus call upon the Christian to be gentle in all his relationships.

Suicide

The word 'suicide' comes the Latin *suicidium* (from *sui caedere*, to kill oneself). Suicide was, in the recent past, a criminal offence and even though it has been decriminalised some people still consider it to be a selfish and dishonourable act. However, most people today are aware that suicide is a mental health issue. It is associated with psychological factors such as difficulty coping with loneliness, depression, shame, pain, stress, or other undesirable situations. A person's perspective becomes distorted and when that person sees no other way out they opt for suicide. Such people need help and hope.

Every suicide leaves many others who are intimately affected by the death; either as a spouse, parent, significant other, sibling, or child of the deceased person. The suicide of a child, for example, may leave not only his/her immediate family to make sense of the act, but also his/her extended family, school community and, indeed, the entire community, struggling to comprehend what has happened.

As with any death; family and friends of a suicide victim feel grief associated with loss. However, suicide deaths leave behind a unique set of issues for the survivors. They are often overwhelmed with psychological trauma and feel guilty and confused. It can be especially difficult for survivors because many of their questions as to the victim's final decision are left unanswered, even if a suicide note is left behind. Moreover, survivors often feel that they should have intervened in some way to prevent the suicide, even if the suicide comes as a surprise and there are no obvious warning signs.

Suicide is generally an act of despair and people with suicidal thoughts need sympathy and support. Suicide could be described as self murder and as such it is a violation of this commandment. However, the person who commits suicide is often severely depressed or distressed. In that condition responsibility is diminished and the bereaved family and friends need comfort and pastoral care. Is suicide a sin? Yes. People need to be told that it is morally wrong. That standard needs to be upheld. However, this is not something that should be stressed with grieving survivors. They need kindness and Christian compassion at such a tragic time. May God help us to minister to those who are affected by such a terrible event!

Assisted Suicide

Regarding 'assisted suicide' the current legal position in Britain is that such activity is illegal. The law states:

> A person who aids, abets, counsels or procures the suicide of another, or an attempt by another to commit suicide, shall be liable on conviction on indictment to imprisonment for a term not exceeding fourteen years.[2]

This law is applicable when a substantial part of the aiding, abetting, procuring or counselling of the suicide occurs in England or Wales. The suicide itself can be committed in any country.

However, this may soon be altered. The Director of Public Prosecutions (DPP) in Britain announced that relatives of people who kill themselves will not face prosecution as long as they act out of compassion and assist only a clear wish to commit suicide.[3] This means that relatives of people who kill themselves will not face prosecution as long as they do not maliciously encourage them and assist only a "clear, settled and informed wish" to die. He outlined guidance to make it easier for those helping someone end their life to know if they might be open to prosecution. The D.P.P. said:

> There are no guarantees against prosecution and it is my job to ensure that the most vulnerable people are protected while at the same time giving enough information to those people like Mrs Purdy who want to be able to make informed decisions about what actions they may choose to take. Assisting suicide has been a criminal offence for nearly 50 years and my interim policy does nothing to change that. There is no immunity from prosecution in these guidelines. We've simply listed the factors that are relevant in a decision whether to prosecute and whether not to prosecute. What's important is to ensure that those who fluctuate in and out of depression or fluctuate in their view about suicide are properly protected. It's got to be a clear and settled wish over a period of time and that's what we'll be looking for in the evidence. The policy is intended to be clear. It's in plain English. If people want

---

[2] Section 2 (1) Suicide Act 1961.
[3] Reported on Channel 4 News, 23 September, 2009.

further advice they should seek that advice from a lawyer or somebody else who can assist.[4]

The law lords, Britain's highest court, asked the D.P.P. to clarify the guidelines surrounding assisted suicide following the case of an individual with multiple sclerosis. This lady asked for clarification on whether or not her husband would face prosecution if he helped her to travel to a clinic in Switzerland to take her own life. The law lords unanimously ruled that this woman had the right to argue that the rules on assisted suicide were unclear.

Launching his interim policy on prosecuting cases of assisted suicide the D.P.P. called for public participation in a public consultation process on the factors he has identified which will be taken into account when considering whether prosecutions will be brought for this offence.

The public interest factors *in favour of prosecution* identified in the interim policy are as follows:

1.   The victim was under 18 years of age.

2.   The victim's capacity to reach an informed decision was adversely affected by a recognised mental illness or learning difficulty.

3.   The victim did not have a clear, settled and informed wish to commit suicide; for example, the victim's history suggests that his or her wish to commit suicide was temporary or subject to change.

4.   The victim did not indicate unequivocally to the suspect that he or she wished to commit suicide.

5.   The victim did not ask personally on his or her own initiative for the assistance of the suspect.

---

[4] Channel 4 News, 23 September, 2009.

6. The victim did not have a terminal illness; or a severe and incurable physical disability; or a severe degenerative physical condition from which there was no possibility of recovery.

7. The suspect was not wholly motivated by compassion; for example, the suspect was motivated by the prospect that they or a person closely connected to them stood to gain in some way from the death of the victim.

8. The suspect persuaded, pressured or maliciously encouraged the victim to commit suicide, or exercised improper influence in the victim's decision to do so; and did not take reasonable steps to ensure that any other person did not do so.

The public interest factors *against a prosecution* include that:

- The victim had a clear, settled and informed wish to commit suicide.

- The victim indicated unequivocally to the suspect that he or she wished to commit suicide.

- The victim asked personally on his or her own initiative for the assistance of the suspect.

- The victim had a terminal illness or a severe and incurable physical disability or a severe degenerative physical condition from which there was no possibility of recovery.

- The suspect was wholly motivated by compassion.

- The suspect was the spouse, partner or a close relative or a close personal friend of the victim, within the context of a long-term and supportive relationship.

- The actions of the suspect, although sufficient to come within the definition of the offence, were of only minor assistance or influence, or the assistance which the suspect provided was as a consequence of their usual lawful employment.

These guidelines constitute the introduction of legalisation on assisted suicide by stealth. The current legal position is that the taking of life by another person is murder or manslaughter. These are among the most serious criminal offences and it seems inappropriate to launch a public consultation process about such a matter. Should our policy (legal or moral) be governed or even guided by considering as many views as possible or should it be determined by the revealed mind of God. For the believer there is only one answer to that. God's Word must be the final arbiter.

It is clear that this new code is a departure from the existing law, in spite of soundings to the contrary from the D.P.P. It sets out a substantial number of factors both for and against prosecution in all types of cases. It assumes that people, under certain circumstances, have the right to assist others in taking their own lives. This is where there is a clear departure from the existing law and more importantly a clear departure from the absolute moral position of God's law. The final arbiter is public opinion and that can be variable from time to time and culture to culture. This will inevitably go the same route as abortion legislation. Abortion was initially permitted in limited and clearly defined circumstances (primarily for therapeutic reasons) but ultimately it led to abortion on demand. The interim policy on assisted suicide paves the way for euthanasia by conceding the principled position, "you shall not kill".

One must question what is actually in the public interest here. There is historical precedent (as in the case of abortion cited above) which suggests that such departures from absolute positions to relative positions act as a catalyst for further change and ushers in a new order. Assisted suicide, though presented as an act of compassion, is actually a violation of the sanctity of life. Ultimately it will contribute to a depreciation of human life. It certainly goes a long way toward bridging the gap between suicide and euthanasia and to deny this is either disingenuous or naïve. These guidelines not only indicate current thinking on this issue but they also move toward the legitimisation of assisted suicide. It is inevitable that existing legislation will be amended to accommodate assisted suicide.

The dilemma about assisted suicide emerges partly from the medical ability to sustain life beyond the point where, in the past, patients would have been allowed to die. We all want our loved ones to die with dignity and we all hope for a good death ourselves. Certainly, there are times when a patient's life should not be prolonged by unnatural interventions. This is a complex and emotive issue often exacerbated by authoritarian regimes in medical institutions. People feel that they should have autonomy and in certain instances this is appropriate. If a person is diagnosed with terminal cancer they should have the right to refuse treatments which may prolong the duration of life but adversely affect the quality of that life. It is not wrong to want to avoid spending your last few months of life in a hospital bed but that is not the same as asking somebody to assist you to take your own life.

Euthanasia

The essential difference between assisted suicide and euthanasia is that in the former a person makes a choice about his/her own death whereas in the latter others make that decision. Medical professionals face many difficult ethical issues. One of the issues facing them, and society in general, is that of euthanasia. Some people (usually atheistic) argue that laws should accommodate 'mercy killing'. They contend that, in certain circumstances, the bringing about of a gentle death in the case of incurable and painful disease is a humane and appropriate response.

This is an emotive issue. None of us want to witness our loved ones suffer. We feel helpless and we suffer (emotionally) in their pain. When that person has a terminal illness and there is loss of mobility, dignity and consciousness we may think a simple injection which brings an end to their life is the solution. But this is very dangerous thinking and raises many ethical and legal issues including the consent of the patient and the role of the doctor. Medical professionals still exercise their judgement about whether or not a person, in certain circumstances, should be resuscitated. It was revealed in a newspaper article recently that: '46% of elderly patients who had the words "do not resuscitate" on their charts were not consulted and in most cases these fateful words were written by relatively inexperienced junior doctors.'[5]

Euthanasia is a huge issue and we are merely touching on it here. Nevertheless we can say that even if the patient has given prior consent to have his life terminated there are still social issues to be addressed. If euthanasia is legalised or accommodated by not prosecuting relatives, friends and medical professionals who assist in this process there may be unforeseen and undesirable outcomes. For example, some patients may feel pressurised to relieve their families or the state of the burden (emotional and financial) of keeping them alive.

There are many pragmatic arguments against euthanasia, such as the fact that pain can now be effectively managed and medicated so that physical suffering is virtually eliminated. It is perfectly legitimate to allow somebody to die. It is acceptable in certain circumstances not to attempt resuscitation. But there is a difference between that and killing people. It is the principled argument against it that is the most compelling. The sanctity of life must be protected.

---

[5] Holmquist, Kate. *The Irish Times*, 19 September, 2009.

In a society where economics is the paramount consideration there is a danger that ultimately even clinical decisions will be primarily determined by financial management policies and professionals. The elderly, the chronically sick and the intellectually and physically disabled would become very vulnerable. It is easy to say that these groups could be protected in law but laws change ultimately by the will of the people. As already stated there was a time when abortion on demand would never have been contemplated by society but now it is for many a form of post-sex contraceptive.

Abortion

This is a huge problem in many countries today. The 1966 U.K. Abortion Act allowed for abortion in limited circumstances such as medical reasons. It envisaged that therapeutic abortion would really be a result or side effect of the medical treatment of the mother. But people have driven a coach and two horses through that piece of legislation and now abortion on demand is the reality and the norm, whatever the small print might say.[6] Only a tiny proportion of the abortions performed are for legitimate 'medical' reasons. The vast majority are for social reasons and come into the category of late birth control. This is an abomination in the sight of the Lord.

This commandment forbids such deliberate and avoidable killing. We should speak up for those who cannot speak up for themselves. We should have compassion for women who have had abortions. I have no doubt that it is emotionally detrimental and damaging to

---

[6] I am not suggesting that women don't experience emotional trauma in coming to a decision to terminate a pregnancy. I acknowledge that in cases of rape and incest many women have agonised about such a choice. I believe that where there are medical complications in a pregnancy, which would threaten the health and life of the mother, abortion can be morally justified.

their mental health. Nevertheless it has to be said that countless millions of babies have been murdered in the womb in our so called 'civilised' societies. The termination of a pregnancy may be acceptable if the mother's health is genuinely at risk but such instances are comparatively few.

Our Thoughts, Words and Deeds

This commandment forces us to recall some of the things we have said or done or thought. Have we harboured and nurtured hatred in our hearts? If we engage in character assassination then we have broken the principle of this commandment. Martin Luther presents us with these challenging words:

> This commandment is violated, not only when he does evil but when he fails to do good to his neighbour. Or, though he has the opportunity, fails to prevent, protect and save him from suffering bodily harm or injury. If you send a person away naked when you could clothe him, you have let him freeze to death. If you see anyone suffer hunger and do not feed him, you have let him starve. It will do you no good to plead that you did not contribute to his death by word or deed for you have withheld your love for him and robbed him of the service by which his life might have been saved. Therefore God rightly calls all persons murderers who do not offer counsel and aid to men in need and in peril of body and life. He will pass a terrible sentence upon them in the Day of Judgment.[7]

And Christ had strong words for those who ignore the hungry, the destitute, the sick and those languishing in prison:

> 'Depart from Me…for I was hungry and you gave Me no food; I was thirsty and you gave Me no drink; I was a stranger and you did not take Me in, naked and you did not clothe Me, sick and in prison and you did not visit Me.' "Then they also will answer Him, saying, 'Lord, when did we see You hungry or thirsty or a stranger or naked

---

[7] Peters, Albrecht. *Commentary on Luther's Catechisms: Ten Commandments,* Concordia Publishing House, 2009.

or sick or in prison, and did not minister to You?' Then He will answer them, saying, 'Assuredly, I say to you, inasmuch as you did not do *it* to one of the least of these, you did not do *it* to Me' (Matthew 25: 41-45).

We can take this commandment and turn it in a positive direction. Not only are we not to kill but we are to love others. We are to be kind and compassionate to others. This commandment challenges us and searches our hearts. We are made in God's image and that is not something to be violated.

Capital Punishment

Does this commandment forbid capital punishment? The answer is it neither forbids it nor requires it. Historically, the execution of criminals and political opponents was used by nearly all societies—both to punish crime and to suppress political dissent. In most places that practice capital punishment today, the death penalty is reserved as punishment for premeditated murder, espionage and treason, or as part of military justice. In some countries sexual crimes, such as rape, adultery and sodomy, carry the death penalty, as do religious crimes such as apostasy (renunciation of the state religion). In many retentionist countries (countries that use the death penalty), drug trafficking is also a capital offence.

In China human trafficking and serious cases of corruption are also punished by the death penalty. In militaries around the world court-martials have imposed death sentences for offences such as cowardice, desertion, insubordination and mutiny.

Among countries worldwide, almost all European and many Pacific Area states (including Australia and New Zealand) have abolished capital punishment. In Latin America most countries have completely abolished the use of capital punishment, while some countries, such as Brazil allow for capital punishment only in exceptional situations, such as treason committed during wartime. Canada has got rid of it but the U.S.A. (the federal government and 36 of the states) retain it.

The majority of democracies in Asia (Japan and India) retain it. In Africa, Botswana and Zambia retain it but South Africa, which is probably the most developed African nation, and which has been a democracy since 1994, does not have the death penalty.

Capital punishment is a contentious issue in some cultures. Supporters of capital punishment argue that it deters crime, prevents recidivism, that it is less expensive than life imprisonment and is an appropriate form of punishment for some crimes. Opponents of capital punishment argue that it has led to the execution of the wrongfully convicted, that it discriminates against minorities and the poor and that it does not deter criminals more than life imprisonment. They argue that it encourages a culture of violence, that it is more expensive than life imprisonment and that it violates human rights.

Does the sixth commandment require the death penalty for murder? Does the sixth commandment forbid the execution of convicted murderers? Capital punishment for murder was part of the judicial law. Let us recall that, as stated earlier, there were three dimensions to the law. First, there was the moral law. Second, there was the judicial law. Third, there was the ceremonial law. It will be helpful here to remind ourselves that the moral law is absolute and applies to all eras and all peoples. In other words it still applies today. This sixth commandment, "you shall not kill", is part of God's timeless moral law. However, the penalty for that crime belongs to the judicial aspect of the law and is, therefore, not necessarily required today. The judicial aspect of the law applied to a particular culture at a specific time in its history. Not all aspects of the law of God are timeless. For example, the ceremonial requirements of the law are no longer relevant because they were fulfilled in Christ. The judicial penalty for murder is a matter for the state. Some will argue that Scripture demands it but that is not so. It is true that Scripture demanded it then and there but that is not to say that it demands it here and now. Understanding the three dimensions of the law (moral, judicial and ceremonial) is the key to unlocking a truly biblical position on this issue.

However, the Bible does not prohibit capital punishment. The penalty commanded by God for murder at that time was death. That is unequivocal. Whether a society wishes to exercise that penalty today is another matter. The death penalty was also imposed for adultery in ancient Jewish society. We cannot say because the death penalty was imposed then that it therefore follows that it should also be imposed now. Who would want those who do not honour their father and mother to be stoned? Stoning to death was the judicial penalty for a breach of the absolute law, "honour your father and mother". In many Muslim countries today people can be stoned to death for adultery. However repugnant adultery may be to our religious sensibilities most decent people would not want to see adulterers executed. In decent society this is considered to be barbaric. Many Christians today are confused about this matter and they think that Scripture demands the death penalty for murder. Sadly they have been misled by their spiritual leaders who do not fully understand the difference between the moral and judicial aspects of the law. They understand how the ceremonial aspect of the law has passed away but fail to separate the moral and judicial elements of the law regarding murder. Yet they have no difficulty separating these two dimensions of the law when it comes to adultery and failure to honour parents because both of these also required the death penalty.

What can be said on this matter, therefore, about countries that exercise the death penalty for the crime of murder? The apostle Paul wrote about the necessity of submitting to government.

> Let every soul be subject to the governing authorities. For there is no authority except from God, and the authorities that exist are appointed by God. Therefore whoever resists the authority resists the ordinance of God, and those who resist will bring judgment on themselves. For rulers are not a terror to good works, but to evil. Do you want to be unafraid of the authority? Do what is good, and you will have praise from the same. For he is God's minister to you for good. But if you do evil, be afraid; for he does not bear the sword in vain; for he is God's minister, an avenger to *execute* wrath on him who practices evil. Therefore *you* must be subject, not only because of wrath but also for conscience' sake. For because of this you also pay taxes, for they are God's ministers attending continually to this very thing. Render therefore to all their due: taxes to whom taxes *are due*, customs to whom customs, fear to whom fear, honour to whom honour (Romans 13:1-7).

The clear implication is that in certain situations it is legitimate for the civil authorities to exercise the sword. Not just brandishing it as a threat but using it as an instrument of execution. The sword is the emblem of death and the authorities, by divine ordination, have that sword placed in their hands.

Nevertheless, it should be pointed out that Christians do not submit to all governments on all matters. Communist countries had laws which forbade the reading and distribution of the Scriptures. These laws were ignored, circumvented and broken by Christians. There are repressive regimes today where Christians do the same and it is not sinful because the laws of these regimes are morally wrong and God's law is a higher law. In a democracy we do not submit passively to the laws of the state, rather we participate in enacting and reforming legislation for the governance of society. Scripture does not demand the death penalty. We do not have to accept the norms of the then culture as normative for us today. Scripture does not oppose slavery but that does not mean that we should be in favour of slavery. Yet that is the very argument of some believers with regard to the death penalty. They are misguided.

Christians disagree on the issue of the death penalty out of ignorance and sometimes because of arrogance. It is a controversial matter. There is no consensus on this issue because there is no clarity about the biblical perspective. So, in the absence of consensus we must try to examine the implications of this commandment, "You shall not murder". In the history of Ireland there were hundreds of offences for which a person could be hanged. There is no way that such a thing can be justified. It was legitimised state execution often for the most trivial of crimes. But Ireland has changed and its laws have changed to reflect that shift to self-government (from colonial rule).

We have already mentioned that none of the European Union countries exercise capital punishment for murder. In fact it is a condition of entry for a country wishing to join the E.U. that the death penalty for murder be abolished. Ireland, like many European countries is a civilised society with its own sovereign laws as well as European legislation which governs its affairs.

Wherever capital punishment is retained it needs to be safeguarded with judicial procedures so as to err on the safe side of caution.

God Himself commanded the death penalty for murder eight to nine hundred years before the commandments were given at Sinai. Immediately after the flood, the Almighty said to Noah, "Whoever sheds man's blood, by man his blood shall be shed" (Genesis 9:6). Some people say that this statute has never been rescinded. But surely we no longer adhere to the eye-for-an-eye and a tooth-for a-tooth principle. A state may exercise it and others may lobby for its abolition. It is at least a good thing that society is reluctant to take a human life and that there is debate about the issue.

It could be argued that the injunction given to Noah was later incorporated in the judicial Law of Moses where it categorically states that the death penalty is the *only* punishment for murder. It could be argued from this that there is no other form of just restitution. The Pentateuch says, 'Whoever kills a person, the murderer shall be put to death on the testimony of witnesses; but one witness is not *sufficient* testimony against a person for the death *penalty*' (Numbers 35:30). Those who argue for the death penalty are not so insistent about the number of witnesses. In this they are inconsistent in expositing Scripture and not being faithful exegetes of the texts. The next verse in Numbers says, 'you shall take no ransom for the life of a murderer who *is* guilty of death, but he shall surely be put to death' (Numbers 35:31). The argument here is that a person should not be able to buy their way out of the sentence. It clearly says the murderer should be put to death but elsewhere, as already pointed out, the death penalty also applied to people for disobeying their parents and in cases of adultery. Consistency of argument would necessitate the reintroduction of capital punishment for disobedient children and adulterers and I don't know of any lobby for this.[8]

Cain

Cain was the first man ever to be born and he murdered his brother Abel. God cursed but did not kill Cain, nor did He allow anybody to kill him. It could be argued that Cain was not put to death probably because of the unique situation as this murder occurred at a crucial juncture in the human race. Early civilisation was to issue from the first offspring of Adam and Eve. Cain was allowed to live, but as a murderer he was cursed of God; henceforth he would exist, but only as a fugitive. The men and women of early civilisation lived to very

---

[8] And I sincerely hope that I don't accidentally kick-start one by my argument!

great ages. He had to flee from place to place as a vagabond because he was a murderer. Every man and woman living at that time knew that he should not have done such a thing. But where did this knowledge come from? The sixth commandment had not been written upon the tablets of stone at this point in history. Neither had this statute been communicated to Noah, for he was not yet born. These commandments, as contained in the Moral Law of God, are creation institutions. The monogamy of marriage, the sacredness of the Sabbath and the sanctity of human life were known from the beginning.

Cain's life was spared but it was not a ruling for all time. Importantly, therefore, we can conclude that some of God's rulings are not intended for permanent duration. God's moral laws, including, "You shall not murder", is enduring and undeviating. The ceremonial aspect of the law has been abolished. Under the judicial aspect of the law murderers were to be put to death for the deliberate killing of another person but this punishment comes under the judicial aspect of the law and that was temporary. Murder is always wrong and a serious violation of God's permanent moral law but the punishment for it came under the Jewish judicial system and that is no longer applicable. Nevertheless murder must be punished severely.

In Ireland it carries a mandatory life sentence but that usually means not more than fifteen years incarceration and many people rightly feel this is too lenient. Many people in Ireland and the U.K. feel that there is too much emphasis on the human rights of the murderer and not enough emphasis on the human rights of the victims and their families. Murder destroys the lives of the victim's family. A person who commits murder is given a certain tariff whereby he is entitled to a Parole Board hearing after a certain number of years (say twelve years). It is the duty of the parole board to decide if that person is still a threat to society or not. If the person, in their opinion, no longer poses a threat then they will be released. Often the murderer is released within fifteen years and this rankles with the families and friends of the victims and is an issue that society on this side of the Atlantic needs to address.[9]

In his defence before Festus, the apostle Paul said, "…if I am an offender, or have committed anything deserving of death, I do not object to dying" (Acts 25:11). Paul readily conceded that if he had done anything demanding capital punishment, then the just punishment should take effect. He did not object to the God-ordained judgment of the death penalty as it pertained in the ancient world. The state today also has the right to exercise the death penalty for murder. But it has the right to *not* execute murderers also.

I have accused the pro capital punishment camp of ignorance and arrogance but it has to be said that the same can be said for the anti capital punishment camp with regard to how they use (or rather abuse) Scripture. This latter group say that the sixth commandment, "you shall not kill", forbids the death penalty. This is a foolish basis for the abolition of the death penalty. The words that Jesus spoke to the Sadducees in a discussion about the resurrection seem apt, "You are mistaken, not knowing the Scriptures" (Matthew 22:29). The section of the Decalogue which states "You shall not murder" does not apply to the punishment required by God in the Jewish judicial system for those who committed murder. This sentence when carried out today is not murder.

---

[9] Sentences for murder in the U.S.A. (where the death penalty is not imposed) are usually much longer than those issued in Ireland and the U.K.

The Seventh Commandment

You shall not commit adultery

The Bible has much to say about lust, uncleanness, fornication and adultery, all of which are forbidden of God. Man's Creator is intrinsically pure and holy. '*You are* of purer eyes than to behold evil, and cannot look on wickedness' (Habakkuk 1:13). In Scripture, lust and uncleanness are broad terms that cover all manner of sexual sins. But adultery and fornication are much more specific, having different meanings. Hebrew, Greek and English dictionaries all make this clear. Fornication is illicit sexual relationships *outside* of marriage. Adultery is illicit sexual relationships *within* marriage. For a married person to have a sexual relationship with another person other than their matrimonial partner is to commit adultery. This seventh commandment is about adultery, involving married persons. Therefore, it is essential that the institution and state of marriage is rightly understood.

Marriage is a divine institution. It was established by God at creation. And the LORD God caused a deep sleep to fall on Adam, and he slept; and He took one of his ribs, and closed up the flesh in its place. Then the rib which the LORD God had taken from man He made into a woman, and He brought her to the man. And Adam said: "This *is* now bone of my bones and flesh of my flesh; she shall be called Woman, because she was taken out of Man." Therefore a man shall leave his father and mother and be joined to his wife, and they shall become one flesh. And they were both naked, the man and his wife, and were not ashamed (Genesis 2:21-25).

Marriage is monogamous. In other words it is a one-man, one-woman relationship for life. It is honourable; for the mutual comfort and blessing of both man and woman. Paul affirms this in his letter to the Ephesians, *'For this reason a man shall leave his father and mother and be joined to his wife, and the two shall become one flesh.'* This is a great mystery, but I speak concerning Christ and the church' (Ephesians 5:31, 32). Marriage is a gift from God which is meant to help us avoid immorality. Paul wrote to the Corinthians, 'because of sexual immorality, let each man have his own wife, and let each woman have her own husband' (1 Corinthians 7:2). Our Lord Himself said:

> "Have you not read that He who made *them* at the beginning *made them male and female*, and said, *For this reason a man shall leave his father and mother and be joined to his wife, and the two shall become one flesh* '? So then, they are no longer two but one flesh. Therefore what God has joined together, let not man separate" (Matthew 19:4-6).

Clearly this is a sacred union where the couple (male and female) is united as such by God the Creator, never to be separated in this world until death. This is clear unmistakable language. No man must have another man's wife and no woman must have another woman's husband. There are to be no rivals; no other lovers. The writer to the Hebrews says, 'Marriage *is* honourable among all, and the bed undefiled' (Hebrews 13:4) and any breach of this is adultery. Many people in our day say that this is the ideal but it's not such a big deal. We live in a fallen world where adultery always has and always will be a fact of life and so we have to live with it. But we should not become so accustomed to it that we begin to see it as normal or acceptable.

This seventh commandment is about a personal and precious family relationship between husband and wife. It needs emphasis in these days when marital breakdown and divorce is becoming more and more frequent. Behind the statistics there is a great deal of pain and heartache. Adultery is a major cause of marital breakdown. It is a violation of a sacred trust which causes distress, broken hearts and broken homes. It causes bitterness that spills over into future generations and leads to much confusion amongst children about relationships.

This generation is particularly prone to break the seventh commandment but it is not a uniquely modern phenomenon. This commandment was given fifteen-hundred years B. C. because it was obviously necessary. The prohibition exists because of our disposition. It is necessary because men and women are inclined to succumb to their basic carnal desires. Adultery is an ignoble thing. It is a betrayal of trust. It is rooted in lust and is a base desire to gratify one's lust. It is insensitive to the dignity of the betrayed partner and is a selfish and callous act.

There have been particularly licentious times in history. Christ described His contemporaries as a "wicked and adulterous generation" (Matthew 16:4). We tend to spiritualise this. This is understandable as the Old Testament prophets frequently used the word 'adultery' in a metaphorical sense for unfaithfulness to God. Nevertheless it can also be literally true of a generation as it is of this present age.

The Bible abhors sin but it describes sinful actions in poignant stories and in it we can read of many lives that were ruined by sins of various kinds. There are numerous instances of people who have violated this commandment recounted in Scripture and the most infamous, in the Old Testament, is that of David and Bathsheba. Before we take a closer look at this sad incident we should note how the Bible deals with sin. It calls it by its name and never side-steps it. Scripture does not use euphemisms ('an affair' or 'a fling'). The Bible does not gloss over issues but neither does it pander to our prurient curiosity. In all the immorality we are never given the sordid, lurid details as in today's magazines and kiss-and-tell biographies and autobiographies. We are spared the gratuitous detail of films which glorify adultery and indulge us. Today's newspapers have the salacious details of celebrity affairs and adulterous activity amongst the high and low in society for its readership. But the Bible is clear that all this is abhorrent and we are never given occasion to feast on the sinful details.

From Desire to Despair

The story of the adulterous relationship between David and Bathsheba is recorded in 2 Samuel 11. One day when David's army was away in battle he was at home walking on the roof of his palace when he saw a woman (Bathsheba) who was bathing. He sent for her and had sex with her and she conceived a child from that union. Her husband was Uriah the Hittite; one of David's best warriors. David initially tried to persuade him to return and be with his wife but Uriah was so loyal that he would not consider leaving his post. So David commissioned his murder. Murder and adultery are often related in the sense that revenge for adultery is often a motive for homicide.

This was a very tragic event in David's life that shows how the brief pleasure of sin was surpassed by the terrible pain of sin. There were catastrophic consequences to his actions. Verse 27 of that chapter says, '...the thing that David had done displeased the LORD'. The incident brought despair to David's soul. He seemed to carry on for a time as if nothing had happened. But it must have been very difficult for him to preside as judge in cases of adultery and murder when he was harbouring guilt for his own adulterous and murderous actions.

David became emotionally and physically ill. In several psalms David mentions this collapse. It ravished his flesh and he lost his health and his friends. He calls out to God, "I am weary with my groaning; all night I make my bed swim; I drench my couch with my tears" (Psalm 6:6).

The adulterous incident was very destructive to his friends. One of David's counsellors was a man named Ahithophel. When the Absalom rebellion broke out Ahithophel joined the conspirators in Absalom's forces. This was a terrible blow to David and he asked God to, "turn the counsel of Ahithophel into foolishness!" But Ahithophel gave evil advice to Absalom. He told him that David had left ten of his women behind in Jerusalem and he advised Absalom to rape them in front of all the people. We might well ask why this wise counsellor would have given such diabolical advice. The answer to that may well have something to do with the fact that he was Bathsheba's grandfather. It would hardly be surprising if the old man hated David for the seduction of his granddaughter and the murder of her husband. This seems like his vengeance.

> Whoever commits adultery with a woman lacks understanding; He *w ho* does so destroys his own soul. Wounds and dishonour he will get, and his reproach will not be wiped away. For jealousy *is* a husband's fury; therefore he will not spare in the day of vengeance. He will accept no recompense, nor will he be appeased though you give many gifts (Proverbs 6:32-35)

It seems that Ahithophel was just biding his time. Then one day David gets news that Ahithophel hanged himself. The tragedy of David's sin had far-reaching effects. One wonders how Bathsheba felt in all of this. Not only is David haunted by the ghost of Uriah but he is now also haunted by the ghost of Ahithophel.

When David was confronted by the Prophet Nathan (2 Samuel 12) his heart broke and he wept openly. He was remorseful but there would be consequences. The effects of adultery are felt in the family.

David's adulterous action was symptomatic of his licentious nature. He took many wives and this was expressly forbidden in Scripture. In this he was a very bad example to others, especially within his own family. The episode with Bathsheba weakened his resolve in dealing with sexual sin within his own family. How could he exercise moral authority when he had flagrantly violated this law himself?

When David's son Amnon raped his own half-sister Tamar, David did nothing about it. So his other son Absalom seeing that his father wasn't going to do anything about it, took the law into his own hands and murdered Amnon. What did David do about that? Nothing! He lost all moral authority in his own home—not even Solomon escaped it for he too was morally corrupt and disobeyed the law of God by taking many wives.

David's adultery brought disaster to his realm. Before the adultery with Bathsheba, David seemed to be invincible. But after the affair he had nothing but trouble with his kinsmen and within the kingdom. This is seen in Absalom's rebellion. Nathan said, "...by this deed you have given great occasion to the enemies of the LORD to blaspheme" (2 Samuel 12:14). On one occasion David was fleeing Absalom. He had gone a short distance beyond the summit of the Mount of Olives when he encountered a man named Shimei of the house of Saul. Shimei cursed David and followed David along the way and threw stones at him. He shouted at David, "now you *are caught* in your own evil, because you are a bloodthirsty man!" (2 Samuel 16:8). It's a pathetic sight; the king being abused in this way. Abishai (one of David's right hand men) wants to cut off Shimei's head but

David would not permit this. All that Abishai could see was a foul-mouthed commoner but David surely reflected on the truth of what Shimei was saying. He had after all been responsible directly for the murder of Uriah and indirectly for the death of Ahithophel.

Absalom's rebellion and death caused great anguish to David. The Absalom rebellion was crushed, thanks to Joab. David went to battle against far superior odds. David wanted Absalom spared and asked his troops to deal gently with him. When messengers brought news of a marvellous victory David asked about Absalom and when he learned that his son was dead he cried, "O my son Absalom — my son, my son Absalom — if only I had died in your place! O Absalom my son, my son!" (2 Samuel 18:33).

David lost the respect of those around him because of the Bathsheba episode. Joab was David's helper. It was Joab who executed the order to arrange for Uriah's death. David is now weeping his heart out instead of rejoicing and the victory was turned to mourning. Joab's disrespect for the king is evident in the tone of his speech to David that day:

> Then Joab came into the house to the king, and said, "Today you have disgraced all your servants who today have saved your life, the lives of your sons and daughters, the lives of your wives and the lives of your concubines, in that you love your enemies and hate your friends. For you have declared today that you regard neither princes nor servants; for today I perceive that if Absalom had lived and all of us had died today, then it would have pleased you well! Now therefore, arise, go out and speak comfort to your servants. For I swear by the LORD, if you do not go out, not one will stay with you this night. And that will be worse for you than all the evil that has befallen you from your youth until now." Then the king arose and sat in the gate. And they told all the people, saying, "There is the king, sitting in the gate." So all the people came before the king. For everyone of Israel had fled to his tent (2 Samuel 19:5-8).

Joab was David's nephew and a murderous and insolent man.

After David had indulged himself with Bathsheba he lost the anointing of God. He had a very special commission from God to lead God's people and to build the twelve tribes into a nation. He was commissioned to destroy Israel's enemies. He feared that he would lose that anointing and prayed that God would not take His Holy Spirit from him (Psalm 51). But God did take the anointing from him, not concerning his person but with regard to his power.

That was the end of David the giant slayer. The victory over Goliath came before Bathsheba but Ishbi Benob came after and there is a stark contrast in both encounters. Goliath came from a family of five giants. When David heard about Ishbi Benob he got out his armour and polished it up and like Samson shorn of his locks he said he would go out as he had done before. But the Spirit of God had departed. In the end Ishbi Benob almost killed David, if it hadn't been for Abishai. David became exhausted and had to be rescued by Abishai:

> But Abishai the son of Zeruiah came to his aid, and struck the Philistine and killed him. Then the men of David swore to him, saying, "You shall go out no more with us to battle, lest you quench the lamp of Israel" (2 Samuel 21:17).

David's anointing was gone and in the flesh he was no match for that giant. He once stayed home and encountered Bathsheba, now he is sent home. There were still three giants thirsting for his blood. He had put on a public exhibition of his weakness in front of the whole army. He never won another victory.

God forgave his sin but there were terrible consequences. He continued to write inspired hymns but never again would he lead God's people into battle against the enemy. Was the adultery worth it? Clearly not!

Christians are too fond of making light of adultery by saying look at how God forgave David. But that only shows an ignorance of biblical history. This incident in David's life had knock-on effects. It comes as a warning to all of us. The consequences of a foolish desire indulged can be far-reaching and very serious. Let the example of our lives be a redeeming truth. We are the bride of Christ and we should not debase the Saviour in this way.

Adultery is off limits as far as the law of God is concerned. It causes harm to families and society and it hurts the one betrayed. In Scripture all immodesty and uncleanness such as lust and adultery are prohibited. Jesus said that whoever even looks at a woman with lust is guilty of adultery. But the Bible does not merely proscribe certain vices, it also prescribes or promotes opposite and corresponding virtues such as purity, integrity, faithfulness and decorum. Scripture tells us what marriage should be. There is a positive thrust in all the commandments. The backdrop to this commandment is marriage and so we need to consider this background a little further.

The Bible is not anti-sex. God is not some kind of prudish killjoy. Marriage was instituted by God. Sex was invented by God. Sex is good, within the context of marriage. The libertine scoffs at this. In a promiscuous society this notion seems outmoded and irrelevant. In Genesis we read, 'And the LORD God said, "*It is* not good that man should be alone; I will make him a helper comparable to him" (Genesis 2:18).

Matthew 1 opens with a genealogy. There we meet a man with a problem that goes to the heart of this issue: Joseph thinks that Mary must have betrayed him. But God reassures him that she has been faithful. They were not husband and wife when Mary conceived by the Holy Ghost but they were engaged to be married.[1] Jesus was

---

[1] Engagement in those days was a much more serious commitment than it is in society today.

born of a virgin but into a marriage relationship. The first miracle performed by Christ was at the wedding feast in Cana, Galilee. So attention is drawn to marriage early on in the New Testament. The epistles have direct teaching about the marriage relationship. At the end of the New Testament heaven is in prospect and one of the images used about the consummation of our relationship with Christ is that of marriage. The mystical union between the church and God is spoken of in marital terms. Thus the church is the bride of Christ and the great celebration in heaven will be the wedding feast of the Lamb. Paul's second letter to the Corinthians speaks by way of illustration about the church, but what lies behind it is a very beautiful picture of marriage purity.

So marriage was ordained by God, it did not evolve from society. Marriage is for most people but not for all. Some will never marry either because they will not have opportunity or because they have chosen celibacy. Jesus touches on this when he is answering questions about grounds for divorce. His response brought some comments from his disciples, "If such is the case of the man with *his* wife, it is better not to marry" (Matthew 19: 10). Then Jesus says:

> "All cannot accept this saying, but only *those* to whom it has been given: For there are eunuchs who were born thus from *their* mother's womb, and there are eunuchs who were made eunuchs by men, and there are eunuchs who have made themselves eunuchs for the kingdom of heaven's sake. He who is able to accept *it*, let him accept *it*" (Matthew 19:11-12).

It is not the universal rule of God that everybody should enter into marriage relationship. It is perfectly proper to remain single if one chooses to do so. Some are genetically predisposed in that way but for others it is an honourable choice. Paul spoke about this to the Corinthians, '…I say to the unmarried and to the widows: It is good for them if they remain even as I am; but if they cannot exercise self-control, let them marry. For it is better to marry than to burn *with passion*' (1 Corinthians 7:8-9).

We have already noted that God said, "It is not good for man to be alone". Marriage was inaugurated by God so that men and women could have companionship, comfort, love and sexual satisfaction in a trusting and secure relationship where there is commitment and faithfulness. 'Faithfulness' is identified as a fruit of the Holy Spirit (Galatians 5:22) and it is something to be admired, cherished, aspired to and cultivated in all our relationships, especially in marriage.

With regard to the issue of procreation, marriage is the proper context into which children should be born.[2] God in his providence does not give everybody children and some couples will choose to not have children.

In our materialistic world weddings are becoming more and more elaborate, expensive and worldly even among Christians. Many people today put the cart before the horse and live together while saving money to cover the cost of the wedding day celebratory banquet. Young people want the fully-furnished house and landscaped garden before their wedding. Many weddings are ostentatious. They are a show where the basic spiritual purpose is overshadowed. Stag nights and hen parties and the wedding reception meal are often drunken revels. And Christians seem to want to sail as close to the wind as possible without the boat turning over. Christian wedding celebrations are frequently a sanitised version of what goes on in the world. The world looks on and says they are not much different from us after all. Certainly marriage is a happy occasion and should be celebrated with joy but the distinctive Christian purpose is not to be obscured.

---

[2] Admittedly not all marriages offer the kind of secure stable relationship that children deserve.

Marriage is a creation ordinance for all and not just for Christians. It is a commitment for life and not just a trial period until someone else comes along. Wedding vows are a sacred oath before God where precious promises are made. The couple agree to commit to each other, "for richer or poorer, in sickness or in health" and that covers all social possibilities and physical circumstances. Marriage is an exclusive relationship where the partners contract to love, comfort and honour each other. Others must not interfere, especially parents. Within the bounds of marriage sexual needs, urges, instincts can be satisfied. We are talking here about natural urges, not improper or perverse things. Modern day 'open marriages' where the married couple consent to having other partners is an abomination to God and a violation of the sanctity of marriage. We should have no hesitation about describing such things as perverse, weird and sinful.

The Bible says that Adam knew his wife Eve. It is a discreet and succinct statement. A modern text would give lurid details as if it was a handbook on how to go about things. God ordained marriage and the biblical teaching about marriage is important in helping us to see adultery for what it is.

Anybody contemplating marriage should become familiar with what the Bible says about it. Why get married at all? Why not call it off when the going gets tough? There are plenty of eligible people out there so why not have a re-run? Many of the icons of society; pop stars, film stars, sportsmen and sportswomen have marriages that are in a mess. What message is this giving? What about homosexuals and lesbians, why shouldn't they get married? The gay lobby has the sympathy of the media and gay marriage is deemed to be a human right.[3] The liberal agenda is opposed to traditional values

---

[3] *De jure* if not *de facto*.

and there are many attacks on marriage. But the Bible directs us on all these issues.

Any form of promiscuity whether heterosexual or homosexual is wrong and sinful. Premarital sex and adultery are both sinful. The fact that they are prevalent in society and accepted as 'normal' does not make them acceptable to God and the norm is not the same as normal.

In the Sermon on the Mount when Jesus said that to look at a woman lustfully was adulterous he was not *expanding* the seventh commandment. Rather he was *explaining* the commandment; that's what a sermon is. He explained it in such a way as to expose the hypocrisy of the Pharisees. Many who have never committed the act are nonetheless guilty. Christians are sometimes accused of having hang-ups about sex. But original sin is not of a sexual nature; that's a wrong idea. Sex is not a taboo subject in the Bible. Sin is powerful and sexual perversion, including marital unfaithfulness, is a consequence of the fall.

Is adultery a worse sin than others? There is no league table and no excuse for any sin. All sin is vile and reprehensible to God. But apart from the spiritual consequences there are devastating family and social consequences to adultery as we have seen in the cameo on David's adultery with Bathsheba.

The Bible has a lot to say about temptation; it is a real, down to earth book with exhortations and warnings. We live in an age which is wicked and adulterous. The media (T.V., newspapers, radio, internet, magazines) offer a visual and verbal diet of sex. If we were to cut sex out of tabloid newspapers we would be left with a seriously mutilated paper. We must be clear about the unambiguous teaching of the Bible on sexual matters, particularly with regard to adultery.

The most unlikely people fall in this area. Psalm 51 is David's penitential prayer. It is an eloquent and poignant poem of contrition. David, the writer of most of the psalms and one of the most marvellous men of God in Scripture, fell. If it can happen to David it can happen to anybody; 'let him who thinks he stands take heed lest he fall' (1Corinthians 10:12). Eminent Christians, including many pastors and missionaries have fallen. Nobody is exempt from this temptation.

Scripture contains warnings, rebukes and exhortations on this issue and it also tells us that there is forgiveness for those who fall. Sodom and Gomorrah are bywords for sexual perversion. Joseph, the son of Jacob, was placed under intolerable temptation when Potiphar's wife tried to seduce him and he went to prison as a result of her lies. He is a great example to those faced with temptation. When Moses descended from Mount Sinai with the tablets of stone, upon which the commandments were written, he discovered Aaron and all the people engaged in a sexual orgy and worshipping a golden calf. Israel was surrounded by nations involved in vile sexual practices and God's people often joined in with their activities:

> Now Israel remained in Acacia Grove, and the people began to commit harlotry with the women of Moab. They invited the people to the sacrifices of their gods, and the people ate and bowed down to their gods. So Israel was joined to Baal of Peor, and the anger of the LORD was aroused against Israel (Numbers 25:1-3).

In Malachi we read about men ditching their wives for younger foreign women.

In the New Testament adulterers are featured, often as recipients of God's gracious forgiveness. Luke 7 records the story of Jesus in the house of Simon the Pharisee when a woman with a notorious sexual reputation wet Jesus feet with her tears and dried them with her hair. This poor fallen woman, forgiven much by Jesus, evidently loved Him much. Romans 1 (second half) describes the sexual sins so prevalent in the pagan world at the time. The people to whom Paul was writing had come from that background. What is very clear from Romans is that sexual sin is an external and evident sign of inward depravity. Paul wrote to the Corinthians:

> Do you not know that the unrighteous will not inherit the kingdom of God? Do not be deceived. Neither fornicators, nor idolaters, nor adulterers, nor homosexuals, nor sodomites, nor thieves, nor covetous, nor drunkards, nor revilers, nor extortioners will inherit the kingdom of God (1 Corinthians 6:9-10).

But praise God he goes on to say:

> And such were some of you. But you were washed, but you were sanctified, but you were justified in the name of the Lord Jesus and by the Spirit of our God (1 Corinthians 6:11).

He's thinking of particular Christian people whom he knows. He is familiar with their personal histories. Chapters 5 and 7 of this same epistle deal, in a plain and forthright way, with church members and their sexual problems. In chapter 5 Paul tells them very explicitly that they are to deal with a man who had taken his own father's wife. Paul recommended that the person be disciplined. And evidently they did as they were told because later Paul exhorts them to restore that person to fellowship (2 Corinthians 2).

1 Corinthians 7 should be read by all married couples. But beware of getting the wrong idea of sanctification by abstaining from sex to move up the moral ladder. Couples may abstain by mutual consent but only for a short period of time. To do otherwise would be to weaken the resolve to resist sexual temptation. In the first-century church there were people with chequered pasts. Galatians 5 identifies sexual sin which ought to be avoided (see also Ephesians 4). In both Galatians and Ephesians the life of the believer in the Spirit is contrasted with a carnal lifestyle. Paul wrote to the Colossians,

'Therefore put to death your members which are on the earth: fornication, uncleanness, passion, evil desire, and covetousness, which is idolatry' (3:5). It's not just the Pauline epistles which contain insight into the past lives of church members. Peter says, '…we *have spent* enough of our past lifetime in doing the will of the Gentiles — when we walked in lewdness, lusts, drunkenness, revelries, drinking parties, and abominable idolatries' (1 Peter 4:3). The second letter of Peter and the book of James contain the same points stated very clearly. In Revelation the personification of all that is evil is described as a whore.

We must understand the awfulness of this sin in the sight of God and not grow accustomed to it. Thankfully there is forgiveness, mercy and restoration. God is able to pick up those who have fallen. Where there is genuine repentance, confession and pleading the merit of the blood of Jesus there is full and complete forgiveness. When God forgives he forgets and the slate is wiped clean. He never throws our history back in our faces. He has cast our sins into the depths of the sea. He has separated them from us as far as the East is from the West. The grace of God is wonderful. In this matter of adultery the grace of God is beautifully illustrated in the New Testament story of the woman caught in the act of adultery which is recorded in John 8:1-12.

The Woman Taken In Adultery

This is a story of compassion and forgiveness. It is also a story that provides insight to the wisdom and discernment of Jesus in dealing with people. Religious leaders were trying to trap Jesus, sometimes concerning the Sabbath, sometimes concerning his views about resurrection. They sought to find contradictions between the teachings of Moses and the teachings of Jesus. They wanted to stir up conflict.

On this occasion Jesus had been teaching in the temple when a woman taken in adultery is brought to Him. Will Jesus agree with Moses about her penalty? Let us examine the case and its consequences. Here is God, the author of the commandments, dealing with a guilty sinner. It is a story which demonstrates God's gracious dealings with a lawbreaker.

A Guilty Woman

If this woman was caught in the act of adultery it begs the question: where is the man who was involved with her? Why is he not in trouble also? However, there is no question about her guilt. She does not plead innocence. She was caught in the act. Being guilty, she is typical of us all (Romans 3:10-23). Jesus does not make light of her misdeed. He does not endorse her behaviour. In spite of the fact that society uses euphemistic terms for this activity, adultery is still adultery. God's standards are unchanging.

A Stooping Man

The text says 'Jesus stooped down and wrote'. We know that the purpose of the accusers was to trap Jesus. If Jesus said, set her free then He would obviously contravene the Mosaic Law. On the other hand if Jesus said she should be stoned He would be heading for a clash with the Roman authorities. According to Roman law the Jews were not permitted to execute anyone. So uppermost in the minds of these religious leaders was the thought that they could trap Jesus by putting Him in an impossible position. Surely He would have to disrespect either the Judaic or Roman Law. It is like a game of chess where "check!" is declared, believing it is only a matter of moments before "check mate!" is acknowledged in their favour.

It is nevertheless interesting that they bring her to Jesus because in doing this they inadvertently concede that Jesus has the authority to preside in judgement on such cases. Jesus stooping down is a picture of how He condescended to save us. What did Jesus write? It was hardly that Jesus was at a loss as to what to say and doodled in the sand to buy some time! Neither is it credible that He merely scribbled in the sand to show his contempt or lack of interest in the question/questioners. Some say that He may have written the names and sins of the people. Maybe He wrote: 'If a man commits adultery with another man's wife - with the wife of his neighbour - both the adulterer and the adulteress must be put to death' (Leviticus 20.10). Maybe He wrote: 'If a man is found sleeping with another man's wife, both the man who slept with her and the woman must die' (Deuteronomy 22:22-24).

These texts call for both parties to be stoned but the male participant was not brought before Jesus which was clearly unjust.[4] Christ's words are astonishing: "Let him without sin cast the first stone" (v.7). By asking for a sinless accuser to initiate her execution Jesus showed them that they were unfit to uphold the Law. Jesus stooped to write again. Maybe He wrote the Ten Commandments. (Exodus 20:1-17). He had once written them in stone with His finger!

Liberated not licensed

Jewish law required the witnesses in any case of capital punishment to begin the stoning. But in this case the accusers leave. The older ones first perhaps because they either had more sins or more sense or both! When we are legalistic and judgemental about the sins of others and we come into the presence of Christ we soon find attention shifted to ourselves. Then Jesus speaks to this woman, "where are your accusers?" She was liberated by Jesus, but she wasn't given a licence to live a licentious life. The woman called Jesus "Lord" (v.11). She was no longer condemned. I wonder if she became a follower

---

[4] Was he, perhaps, a single man and she a married woman?

of Christ. The pointing fingers of religious hypocrites brought her to be condemned but she found compassion in the helping hands of Jesus. He defeated her wily accusers and in this there is a beautiful picture of the glorious truth that the accuser of the saints, in spite of all his craft, will ultimately be defeated.

We are most unlikely to make such life/death decisions but we may very well be asked to comment on some moral dilemma. Some people love to try to catch the Christian out. The seventh commandment says, "You shall not commit adultery". That is the only valid Christian position on this issue but let us be compassionate without compromising this divine law.

The Eighth Commandment

You shall not steal

The simplicity of this commandment is striking. It contains only four words. When the national parliament passes legislation it has to go through several stages involving much debate. Eventually a law can be entered on the statute books with many qualifying phrases, restrictions, exceptions, clauses and sub-clauses. Human laws are complicated and frequently certain paragraphs have to be read in the light of other sections of an Act. This is typical of the law which is a specialised area of knowledge. It has become so complex that experts (solicitors, barristers, lawyers, judges) are required to deal with it. Our legislation is convoluted but God's laws are clear. In our legal systems laws are subject to interpretation in the lower courts and reinterpretation in the higher courts. There are supreme courts which have the final authority to pronounce a verdict. Such courts sometimes overturn the decisions of lower courts. But here is God's law: simple and sacred, "You shall not steal". There is no qualification or elaboration in this uncomplicated command.

The Eskimos or Inuit people have many words for *snow* because there is a lot of it in their world. We have a lot of words for stealing for the same reason: there is a lot of it about. We talk of theft, burglary, larceny, mugging, shoplifting, pilfering and robbing. We talk of con jobs, swindling, rackets, scams the misappropriation of funds, fraud and embezzlement. These terms have quite specific meanings. They are not all merely synonyms for theft. They are nuanced words and many have particular legal definitions.

We have burglar alarms in our homes and alarms in our cars. We have insurance against theft for our property. Security cameras and all sorts of precautions are necessary to protect ones property against theft. The police are kept busy trying to solve crimes involving theft. There are people who make their living from stealing. There are professional gangs involved in this field of activity. Many people who are addicted to drugs are involved in crimes of this nature in order to feed their habit. In general it is evident that there is much breaking of this commandment in society. When families are attending funerals their homes can be burgled. Recently a seven year old was found with the church collection in her socks.

Millions are spent by big stores to prevent shoplifting. They hire security firms or employ their own security personnel. They have to write off a certain percentage of their profits because they know that a proportion of their trade is going to be lost through theft. This is an endemic problem in society. God says that it is wrong.

To steal is to take what does not belong to you: that to which you have no right because it is the property of somebody else. The individual commandments are not isolated, rather they are interrelated. For example if we fail to adhere to the first commandment, "You shall have no other gods before Me" then the likelihood of worshipping statues and icons is greatly increased, thus breaking the second commandment. Furthermore, it could be said that even Christians steal from God when they won't give Him the one day in seven that is rightly His. When we are giving money to the church or to missions we should not have a minimalist attitude by thinking, how little can I give to cover my obligation here? Our giving is not measured by what we have given but by what we have left. Breaches of the seventh commandment, "You shall not commit adultery", could be understood as stealing because it is wrongfully taking another person's husband or wife. There is a relationship between this eighth commandment, "You shall not steal" and the tenth commandment, "You shall not covet…" Coveting is to desire greatly what belongs to another person and this has led many people to steal. Sometimes people will murder another person so they can take their possessions. At the root of this there is greed and at the root of that there is a lack of contentment. If we covet another man's, wife, possessions or lifestyle we are guilty of breaking the law even if we have not slept with his wife, stolen his goods or burned his house down. But covetousness often leads to stealing. They are interrelated so that the breaking of one leads to the breach of another.

Specifically, with regard to this commandment, "You shall not steal" we need to ask, what gives rise to it? This has been partly answered already by identifying, discontentment, covetousness and greed. People steal when they are discontent with what God has given in his providence to provide for their care in life. Theft is sometimes committed by those who are unwilling to do anything productive and legal (work) that would lift them out of the circumstances they find themselves in. The attitude is, why bother working if you can take it without effort? Why bother to exert yourself if you can get it the easy way? Paul told the Thessalonians to, 'aspire to lead a quiet life, to mind your own business, and to work with your own hands' (1 Thessalonians 4:11). It doesn't take much intelligence to work out the background. There were those who didn't work and were idle. Consequently they lacked money and they were tempted to be dishonest and Paul says the answer to this is to work. In his second letter to this church he was more explicit, 'For even when we were with you, we commanded you this: If anyone will not work, neither shall he eat' (2 Thessalonians 3:10). We learn from this that Paul also told them this face to face when he was with them and that he is now, once again, reminding them of this.

There were workers and shirkers in the Thessalonian church. Some were sponging on the kindness of other people. It wasn't that they *couldn't* work. That is a different matter. They *wouldn't* work. This verse does not refer to people who are unemployed but are nevertheless actively seeking gainful work. Nor does it refer to people who find themselves in difficult economic circumstances within a community where there is no work for them to do. But even in such a situation the person could possibly get involved in voluntary work or retraining or further education in order to be more employable. A person may need to migrate or emigrate in order to have the dignity of work and become self-sufficient and not always dependant on others. It is not right to accept unemployment benefit from the state unless one is engaged in actively seeking employment. To do so is stealing. This verse does not apply to those with a disability which prevents them from working. But even in these two types of cases such people can contribute something from their social welfare entitlements towards their upkeep. Some people are malingerers or just bone idle and will not work if others continue to feed them. Paul says that supporting them is not the Christian thing to do.

The New Testament gives insight into the remarkable success and wonderful power of the gospel. There were all sorts of people from all ranks of society and many had colourful pasts. Paul is practical and down to earth in his advice, 'Let him who stole steal no longer, but rather let him labour, working with *his* hands what is good, that he may have something to give him who has need' (Ephesians 4:28). They obviously had some converted thieves in their congregation. This also tells us that when a person is converted there isn't an automatic cut off from the old temptations. The advice is clear; a man must work instead of taking what doesn't belong to him and he should become a contributor. To contribute to the needs of others is a complete reversal of that old order.

The book of Proverbs is wise, perceptive and pithy and it touches on many of the commandments. But in relation to this eighth commandment, "You shall not steal", there is a verse which is quite pertinent: 'Give me neither poverty nor riches — Feed me with the food allotted to me; lest I be full and deny *You*, and say, "Who *is* the LORD?" Or lest I be poor and steal, and profane the name of my God' (Proverbs 30:8-9). There is great temptation in both of those extremes. When a person is poor and destitute the temptation to steal may be very strong. When a person is very wealthy it is easy to be ungodly by being obsessed with the treasures of this world. God cares for the poor and that compassion should be reflected in and through our churches.

The harvest practice in the Old Testament is identified in Leviticus:

> "When you reap the harvest of your land, you shall not wholly reap the corners of your field, nor shall you gather the gleanings of your harvest. And you shall not glean your vineyard, nor shall you gather *every* grape of your vineyard; you shall leave them for the poor and the stranger: I *am* the LORD your God" (19: 9-10).

This was a practical way of demonstrating the love of God. And this harvest principle should be practiced by God's people everywhere. The very next verse says, 'You shall not steal, nor deal falsely, nor lie to one another' (19:11). There are many injunctions in the New Testament about assisting the poor.

Stealing is dishonest but honesty is a good thing. Proverbs says, 'Honest weights and scales *are* the LORD's; all the weights in the bag *are* His work' (Proverbs 16:11). Scales these days are electronic and computerised but when I was a boy the shopkeepers used physical weights on balance scales.[1] It was possible to fiddle the scales. That happened in the Old Testament. Leviticus has very explicit instruction about just weights and balances:

> You shall do no injustice in judgment, in measurement of length, weight, or volume. You shall have honest scales, honest weights, an honest ephah, and an honest hin: I am the LORD your God, who brought you out of the land of Egypt. (Leviticus 19:35-37).

God clearly forbids the use of dishonest standards when measuring length, weight or quantity. What is even more interesting about these verses is the way they draw attention to the covenant relationship between God and His people. In this God is saying He is just and honest and therefore His people should be like Him. God's covenant people should reflect true standards. To manipulate the scales is to defraud or steal.

There are people who check measuring instruments to ensure that the customer is getting exactly what he is paying for. So that when we pay a certain price for a litre of fuel for our cars we are actually getting a litre. They check these instruments to ensure they are functioning properly and delivering what they say they are delivering. But they also check to make sure that these instruments have not been manipulated to defraud the public. This is specialised and technical work where specific training is required for people with technical aptitude. It involves also checking the computer software which drives these instruments to ensure that it has not been tampered with or reprogrammed. It is a fact of life that people will cheat if they can get away with it and the fact that such experts are needed to monitor measuring instruments is an indication of our belief that if left unchecked there will be abuse in this area. Overcharging is the modern equivalent of manipulating the scales and it is stealing.

---

[1] In many countries these kinds of scales are still used, especially in open air markets where they are more suitable than electronic scales.

This commandment is about honesty and integrity. There are contemporary relevant issues which need to be addressed in the light of this unequivocal command of God. For example, with regard to computers can we say we have paid for all the software? If the manufacturers found that we were not compliant they would seek compensation or even take us to court. That would be embarrassing and humiliating for many people who do not think of themselves as thieves.

Do we pay our television license? Are we illegally downloading music or movies from the internet? It does not matter if everybody is doing it. Is it right and honest? Are the producers, publishers, distributors, artists and writers getting what they are entitled to or are we bypassing the law and effectively stealing from them? We might be tempted to say nobody knows, but God knows. We might feel these people have enough but that is no excuse for stealing from them. We need to audit ourselves in this regard to be sure we are not in breach of copyright law. Churches, for example are obliged to pay for the hymns they use and need to buy a license. If a church uses a television to show DVD's it must have a T.V. license. We cannot simply dismiss these things as petty. It won't seem petty if we end up in court with a conviction and a large fine, especially if the church is identified in the press.

We are very sharp when we are on the suffering end of being cheated. If we get short-changed when we buy something we are quick to point out the mistake. But does it work the other way around? If we are given too much do we tend to see their misfortune as our good fortune? Do we keep it or take it back?

Kleptomania

Human beings are complex creatures and sometimes there can be psychological reasons for a person's wrongdoing. This does not diminish the sin or crime. Not all sins are crimes and Christians need to evaluate the law in relation to these commandments. In a society where abortion and adultery are not crimes we need to differentiate, on the basis of God's Word, what is moral and immoral. Secular law has drifted away from the true standard of Scripture.

One of the words for stealing which was not included in the list earlier in this chapter is 'Kleptomania'. Kleptomaniacs are people who have a persistent tendency to steal items. Often these objects are not needed for personal use and are not stolen for their monetary value. These people have psychological problems and are usually treated leniently by the courts. They take things despite the fact that they are typically of little value to them. Often Kleptomaniacs could have afforded to pay for the items they steal. Frequently they give away or discard the stolen goods. In this way they are different from shoplifters, even though they may both rob the same thing from exactly the same place. A kleptomaniac experiences feelings of pleasure, gratification or relief when committing the theft. Occasionally the kleptomaniac will hoard the stolen objects or even surreptitiously return them. They usually do not plan the thefts or fully take into account the chances of apprehension and the stealing is done without collaboration with others. These people have an irresistible inclination to steal and will often throw away the stolen goods, as they are mostly interested in the stealing itself. This recurrent failure to resist stealing impulses is often unrelated to financial circumstances.

People with kleptomania often have another psychiatric disorder, such as a mood disorder like depression or anxiety. There is indirect evidence linking it with abnormalities in the brain chemical, serotonin. Nevertheless their actions constitute a violation of this commandment, "You shall not steal". There are different degrees of seriousness with theft crimes such as mugging and pilfering. The judge can decide what punishment fits the crime. In the Old Testament law the Scriptures that discuss theft show a very balanced and graded approach to dealing with the various manifestations of this sin.

There are obvious and less obvious violations of this commandment perpetrated by many in society. For some it is a way of life. For others it is a bad habit. There are those who steal in a crude way but then there are sophisticated thieves; white collar workers who fraudulently balance the books. There are wealthy and well respected business people who made their fortune not by exploiting an opportunity but by exploiting people.

Systems and Structures

There are systems and structures within society and between nations which are inherently unjust and exploitative. Christianity is not just about personal piety. Is our standard of living as a nation based on the exploitation of others? Is there anything we can do about it? Yes. We can pay more for imported products like 'Fair Trade' goods and ask our politicians to put fair trade (and other similarly branded goods) on the political agenda. That is a start. This principle, "You shall not steal" applies to corporations and nations as well as individuals. Many people who consider themselves decent, law-abiding citizens break this commandment by their denial of or indifference to these serious social issues.

We are called to repent of our sins and that involves acknowledging our wrongdoing, asking for forgiveness and determining, by God's grace to forsake those sins. If we steal, there is forgiveness from God and genuine Christian people will also demonstrate forgiving attitudes.

The Ninth Commandment

You shall not bear false witness
against your neighbour

There is a passage of Scripture in the New Testament which speaks of the untameable human tongue; how powerful and dangerous it can be. This passage tells us that we will be judged by what we say. It is an exhortation for believers to exercise control over their speech because words are potentially very destructive. As we consider this ninth commandment it will be instructive to look at that portion of the Word of God as it conveys in vivid terms the powerful influence of the tongue and the perversity of that organ of speech:

> For we all stumble in many things. If anyone does not stumble in word, he *is* a perfect man, able also to bridle the whole body. Indeed, we put bits in horses' mouths that they may obey us, and we turn their whole body. Look also at ships: although they are so large and are driven by fierce winds, they are turned by a very small rudder wherever the pilot desires. Even so the tongue is a little member and boasts great things. See how great a forest a little fire kindles! And the tongue *is* a fire, a world of iniquity. The tongue is so set among our members that it defiles the whole body, and sets on fire the course of nature; and it is set on fire by hell. For every kind of beast and bird, of reptile and creature of the sea, is tamed and has been tamed by mankind. But no man

> can tame the tongue. *It is* an unruly evil, full of deadly poison.
> With it we bless our God and Father, and with it we curse men,
> who have been made in the similitude of God (James 3:2-9)

It is clear from this text that the tongue is difficult to control. Nevertheless self-control is listed as a fruit of the Holy Spirit (Galatians 5:23) and so it is important for us to strive to exercise self-restraint, especially in our speech. James rightly points out that everybody makes mistakes and therefore we are all guilty of sin by virtue of the things we have said. We have all sinned (Romans 3:23) in thought, word and deed.

James illustrates the dominant influence of the tongue by the practice of putting bits in the mouths of horses to make them obey us. The point is that although a horse is a powerful animal it is controlled by a small instrument in its mouth. A small bit can turn the whole animal. So a person who can control the tongue can control his entire being.

The second illustration concerning the influence of the tongue is the rudder of a ship. This small blade at the end of the tiller is able to steer the vessel wherever the pilot wishes it to go. Considering the relative size of the ship and the great force of the wind, the rudder, like the tongue, exerts a powerful influence for an instrument of its size. Powerful orators have altered the destinies of nations for good or bad.[1] Words of praise and encouragement from parents and teachers have positively shaped the lives of many by stimulating and inspiring them to greatness. Words of criticism, scorn and abuse have negatively moulded men and women so that they lack confidence, underachieve and live with feelings of inadequacy all their lives.

The injurious potential of the tongue is graphically pictured by a forest fire. Thousands of acres of valuable woodland can be

---

[1] Such as Martin Luther King and Adolph Hitler, respectively.

destroyed by a single spark. It can result in the loss of animal and human life. In the first two illustrations horses and ships are governed by small objects. In the last picture a great forest is destroyed by a small spark. Similarly, the tongue can either control or destroy. Inflammatory words have destroyed families, neighbourly relations and international relations. Where diplomacy fails war prevails. Words can ignite churches and cause divisions. Words can kindle hatred that is hard to quench. The tongue is involved in many sins where people lie and deceive.

James is not really talking about that piece of flesh in our mouths which is called the tongue, which physiologically assists in speech and enables us to taste. James is referring to the mind that engages the tongue as its means of intelligent communication. Our inability to tame the tongue is an indication of our perverse fallen nature. Mankind was given dominion over all the creatures of the earth and although we have retained this we have lost dominion over ourselves. When James says that 'no man can tame the tongue' he is saying that we are incapable, by our own human power, of subduing our perverse nature. In a degenerate condition the tongue is full of venom and needs the regenerate controlling influence of the Holy Spirit. But James says that Christians are inconsistent and articulate both praise to God and profanities with the same instrument of speech. The bitterness of our hearts and the prejudices of our minds will make us speak evil of others. But this is not right and we must work toward a more God-glorifying verbal Christian witness to the truth.

This ninth commandment says, "You shall not bear false witness against your neighbour". It is a serious offence to lie about another person or misrepresent someone. A person's good name and reputation can be damaged or destroyed by such action. That is why civilised societies have libel laws and legal safeguards and courses of redress concerning allegations of defamation. Witnesses in a court of law are asked to swear that their testimony will be, "the truth, the whole truth and nothing but the truth". There are penalties for breaching this solemn public and legal vow. If falsehoods and lies are told in court it is considered to be perjury and the offender may be publicly reprimanded by the judge, fined and/or imprisoned. It is an offence to lie to the police when they are investigating a crime and the person who does this can be charged with attempting to pervert the course of justice. This commandment has immediate application in a legal context. Deuteronomy elaborates:

> If a false witness rises against any man to testify against him of wrongdoing, then both men in the controversy shall stand before the LORD, before the priests and the judges who serve in those days. And the judges shall make careful inquiry, and indeed, *if* the witness *is* a false witness, who has testified falsely against his brother, then you shall do to him as he thought to have done to his brother; so you shall put away the evil from among you. And those who remain shall hear and fear, and hereafter they shall not again commit such evil among you (19:16- 20)

This shows us the seriousness of the issue. We might never find ourselves in a courtroom answering charges of libel, defamation or slander. We might not ever by guilty of perjury or attempting to pervert the course of justice. We might not even intentionally lie about others but we need to be careful what we say. We must not be careless in this regard. We must avoid gossip. We must not breach confidentialities. We must endeavour at all times to be truthful, especially when speaking about other people. A false accusation can be detrimental to a person's life and livelihood.

Miscarriage of Justice

I recently read a newspaper report about a thirty-four year old man who was wrongly convicted of sexually assaulting a ten-year-old girl. He had his conviction declared a miscarriage of justice. His conviction was overturned after the girl, admitted nine years later that she had made up the allegation. The Court of Criminal Appeal granted the certificate, describing the case as an alarming and disturbing one. The court heard there was a history of animosity between his family and his alleged victim's family (who were neighbours) relating to disputes between rights of way and land. The girl's allegation of sexual assault was made in detailed terms. However, nine years later she admitted that she had made up the allegation. Her guilty conscience compelled her to put the record straight. Understandably, the gentleman in question was pleased and relieved that his conviction had been quashed and that the court had confirmed he suffered a miscarriage of justice. He said he had to live with the stigma of a conviction and he hopes that lessons could be learned and that more care would be taken in the future to ensure it did not happen again. Surely God gave us good advice when He said, "You shall not bear false witness against your neighbour".

God is Truthful

God invariably speaks the truth. Several verses in the New Testament confirm this. The book of Titus speaks of the 'God, who cannot lie' (1:2). Hebrews states, 'it *is* impossible for God to lie' (6:18). In Revelation God is called 'Faithful and True' (3:14; 19:11) because that is His name and nature.

Chinese writing is quite different to English. It does not have the twenty-six letters of our alphabet. Rather it consists of ideograms. These are characters or pictures symbolising a thing or representing something. The ideogram for *faithful* is very interesting. It is the figure of a man and beside his mouth a number of squiggles which represent spoken words. In other words it is a picture of a man standing by what he says. Thus he is seen as dependable and truthful. That is what faithful means and we are to be faithful witnesses to the truth, of the gospel and to the truth in general terms. The Bible is true (John 17:17). Jesus is the truth (John 14:6).

This commandment says, "You shall not bear false witness against your neighbour". How do we define *neighbour*? We are not to limit the scope of application by restricting it to a confined geographical locality within a certain radius of our homes. That would be a perverse interpretation. We cannot say that because so-and-so is not my neighbour I have the liberty to bear false testimony against him without breaking this command. A smart lawyer put questions to Jesus, "Teacher, what shall I do to inherit eternal life?" (Luke 10:25). Jesus asked him what was written in the law and what his interpretation of it was. The man was able to sum up the commandments, "*You shall love the LORD your God with all your heart, with all your soul, with all your strength, and with all your mind,' and 'your neighbour as yourself*" (v.27). Jesus commended him for his knowledge and instructed him to practice it. But the man did not leave the matter there and asked a further question, "And who is my neighbour?" (v.29). So Jesus told the parable of the Good Samaritan and asks, "which of these three [Priest, Levite or Samaritan] do you think was neighbour to him who fell among the thieves?" (v.36). The expert of the law replied, "He who showed mercy on him" (v.37) Jesus replied, "Go and do likewise" (v.37).

The obvious implication for this man was that he should demonstrate loving mercy to non-Jews. He should reach out to those outside covenant relationship with God. The Jews hated Samaritans. For us the application is clear; we too must reach out to our enemies in mercy and love and practical ways. Our religious identity and duties should not prevent us from this. It must have sounded as affronting, absurd and unworkable then as it does now. This is the message of Christ. No doubt there will be those who are well versed in the Scriptures who resent it still. Communities that are hostile to each other often live side-by side. We are clearly commanded by God not to bear false witness, even against our enemies.

Why do people tell lies? Because they think it is to their advantage! This is one sin we have probably all committed. We think a lie will get us out of an awkward corner. Perhaps people lie in order to pander to their pride. A person might say something that isn't true and other gullible people believe it and the liar goes up in their estimation. Perhaps people lie when they are in trouble, to escape difficulty. We can lie when we exaggerate and misrepresent. The New Testament church was full of people who had been liars and were being instructed not to lie anymore, 'Therefore, putting away lying, *'Let each one of you speak truth with his neighbour,'*for we are members of one another' (Ephesians 4:25). And again in Colossians Paul says, 'Do not lie to one another, since you have put off the old man with his deeds' (Colossians 3:9). It is important for Christians to be truthful because God is truthful and we must become more like Him, by His transforming grace.

Have you ever watched a film or read a book which has a courtroom drama scene? When watching or reading such a work of fiction we willingly suspend our disbelief and get caught up emotionally in the drama. We can feel distressed when somebody is bearing false witness against an innocent person who is accused of a crime. The person's life or liberty is at stake and we don't want to see an injustice being done because of the false testimony of somebody bearing witness. We want the opposing counsel to cross-examine and expose the lie in the interest of fairness. We feel a sense of outrage when a decent person is misrepresented and endangered by false witness.

In the novel (and film), *To Kill A Mocking-Bird*, by Harper Lee, Mayella Ewell bears false testimony against a black man named Tom Robinson for a crime he did not commit. She accused him of raping her. It is a terrible thing made all the worse by the fact that he was a good man who had helped her. As we read we want the truth to come out. In that case there was a tragic miscarriage of justice. Tom was found guilty by a prejudiced, all-white jury and subsequently killed while trying to escape custody. Although such things, unfortunately, really do happen, this is nevertheless a work of fiction.

One such true event in history is recorded, when a kind and good man was arrested. False accusations were made and on that basis a conviction was secured. He was tortured and executed. That man's name was Jesus. When He was interviewed by Pontius Pilate He said, "For this cause I was born, and for this cause I have come into the world, that I should bear witness to the truth" (John 18:37). Pilate asked contemptuously, "What is truth?" (v.38). This was not a sincere attempt to discover the truth. Pilate did not want to discuss the issue with Jesus. Here we witness the Roman procurator (regional head of their great legal system); the governor of the province in Judea asking, "What is truth?" It was his task to see that justice was administered in accordance with the law. Here we see the earthly judge before the judge of all the earth and what an absolute contrast it is. Jesus, the one who not only spoke the truth but was truth incarnate, was condescendingly dismissed.

Another form of lying is when people profess to speak in the name of God but what they say is not true. This was true of the religious leaders in Christ's day and it is still true today. Jesus gave these people a ferocious tongue-lashing

> "You are of *your* father the devil, and the desires of your father you want to do. He was a murderer from the beginning, and does not stand in the truth, because there is no truth in him. When he speaks a lie, he speaks from his own *resources*, for he is a liar and the father of it. But because I tell the truth, you do not believe Me. Which of you convicts Me of sin? And if I tell the truth, why do you not believe Me? He who is of God hears God's words; therefore you do not hear, because you are not of God" (John 8:44-47).

This is strong stuff! Jesus told these religious leaders that they were children of Satan. This is not the sanitised Christ that many religious leaders today would want to present. They present a holy but harmless Jesus who is always nice and kind and considerate of other people's feelings. They present a Christ who would never say hurtful things, especially about other religious people. These sanctimonious listeners were outraged by Christ's words and tone. On another occasion He called them a brood of vipers. Yet again He told them that though they appeared holy they were in fact like the inside of a tomb that stank of decomposing flesh. Wow! 'Gentle Jesus, meek and mild' He was not. Jesus didn't conceal His hatred of these people. Some people will recoil at the suggestion that Jesus hated anybody but He did and He still does. Why did He hate them? He hated them because they misrepresented Him. They distorted the truth. Essentially they bore false witness about God.

When we unpack this commandment we see that it is possible to lie by exaggerating. People can distort the truth by adding to it, inflating it or embellishing it. Sometimes people do the opposite by taking away from the truth or minimising something in the way it is presented. Sometimes people don't want the whole truth to be known. Gossiping often adds a bit of untruth about somebody. This is bearing false testimony against one's neighbour. Without ever speaking a word, when a person's name is mentioned, we can convey a certain false impression about somebody in a non-verbal way by our facial expressions and gestures. We can bear false witness against our neighbour by innuendo when we don't quite say something false but we nevertheless imply it. The press can misrepresent people by quoting them out of context or deliberately using a partial quote to present somebody in a particular light. I'm sure we all have some repenting to do in the light of this commandment.

The Tenth Commandment

*You shall not covet your neighbour's house; you
shall not covet your neighbour's wife,
nor his male servant, nor his female servant,
nor his ox, nor his donkey, nor anything
that is your neighbour's*

Jesus, in one section of the Sermon on the Mount (Matthew 6:19-34), tells us to store up treasures in heaven. Here He also talks about the lamp of the body. He is not talking about our physical eyesight but rather our perception. He says that if we are pure of heart we will be satisfied and positive but if we are corrupt we will be dissatisfied and negative. This is a sermon that has echoed throughout two millennia and the message is the same for those who hear it today as it was for those gathered on that hillside long ago. In this sermon Jesus is reminding people that they are spiritual beings and He places great emphasis on the soul. He is telling us that we are pilgrims in this transient world. It is a reminder that we are not merely flesh and blood. He tells us that we should not be materialistic or greedy and He points to the fact that material wealth can hinder spiritual prosperity. Jesus tells His hearers not to be preoccupied (anxious and fretful) about their physical needs but rather to be more occupied with spiritual things.

It is a clear, simple and explicit command. Some of the commandments have specific actions in mind, like, adultery, murder and theft but this commandment is not like that because it concerns itself with thoughts rather than deeds. In this sermon Jesus does refer to adultery and murder, not just as evil actions but as evil thoughts such as lust and hatred.

This tenth commandment tells us not to covet and as such it deals with consuming desires or obsessions to possess what other people have. It deals with jealousy of others especially in relation to their belongings. Thoughts often express themselves in actions. Several of the other commandments are covered in this. Theft begins with coveting another person's property. Adultery begins with coveting another person's wife or husband.

All the commandments have contemporary relevance and here in this command, not to covet, certain greedy attitudes of mind are being condemned. But so too a certain contented attitude of mind is being commended. It is very comprehensive and like all the commandments is relevant irrespective of culture, creed or class. We are not to crave anything that belongs to our neighbour whether it is their property or prosperity.

In a consumerist culture marketing and advertising is designed to create desires so that we want to buy things we can't afford. It's a 'have it now and pay later' society. But people are deceived if they think that contentment is found in material possessions. The quest for contentment is found only in God. People are discontent and they don't know why. It is because they are not at peace with God. Contentment is elusive and unobtainable for those who search for it in thrills and things that can be bought.

Ecclesiastes

Solomon wrote three books of the Bible: the Song of Songs, Proverbs and Ecclesiastes. Ecclesiastes is a book of despair written by a man who had many regrets. Solomon was not happy. This may be surprising considering that he had vast wealth. Solomon had everything he wanted but he learned that neither position nor power nor prosperity nor anything else under the sun could bring contentment.

Cecil Rhodes was one of Great Britain's most illustrious sons. As a young man he went out to South Africa to make his fortune. At the age of twenty-seven he had founded the De Beers Mining Company. Within eight years he controlled all the diamond mining industry in South Africa. At the age of thirty-six he became Prime Minister of the Cape colony (Rhodesia). By the time he was forty-one he not only controlled all of South Africa's diamond mining but he also controlled all its gold mining. I suppose he was the richest man in the world in his day. His legacy to the British Empire on his death was North and South Rhodesia, a tract of territory in Africa equal to the size of France, Germany and Spain together. Cecil Rhodes was a personal friend of General Booth, the founder of the Salvation Army, perhaps one of the poorest men in the world of his day. So the story goes that one day the two men were travelling in a train together and Booth asked Rhodes, "Are you a happy man?" To which Rhodes replied, "No!" He too had learned that true contentment was not to be found in material things.

Solomon shows us that the values of the worldly-minded are futile. When we consider the brevity of life and the length of eternity it puts our brief sojourn on this earth into perspective. However illustrious one's life may appear to be (when judged by one's accumulated wealth) it is worth nothing in eternity. The only treasure we can take to heaven is a redeemed soul. Solomon was a wise man and he shows us from personal experience, observation and deduction that a life lived without God is empty and meaningless. He tells us that there is no point or purpose in anything if we are only going to live for the things and thrills of this world. The person who lives only for what this world has to offer is a lost soul.

Solomon was an incredibly wealthy king of a great commercial empire. He had an export and transportation network second to none, with ships and caravans of camels which supplied distant markets. The wealth of the world flowed into his warehouse. He had the Midas touch so that whatever he touched turned to gold. He was a tremendous success. But material success did not ultimately satisfy him.

Solomon had wide-ranging experience. He was a teacher and a writer. He was an intellectual without peer in his day. Many famous and influential people, including the Queen of Sheba, came from the ends of the earth to listen to his instruction and gain insight. But this fame did not ultimately satisfy him.

Solomon indulged in every sensual pleasure and enjoyment imaginable. He abandoned himself to the gratification of the lusts of the flesh. His harem was enormous, his resources were boundless and his revelry was unrestrained. But this hedonistic lifestyle did not ultimately satisfy him either.

This tenth commandment, "You shall not covet…" speaks to people who are obsessed with material prosperity when they ought to be more concerned with spiritual posterity and the eternal riches they can leave to succeeding generations. We are engineered for eternity not for time and this should enable us to put a higher value on the things of God and to prefer them to the things of this world.

Thomas Chalmers was an unconverted minister of religion in Scotland but he had an ambition to be professor of maths at Edinburgh University. Prior to his conversion he wrote a pamphlet in which he stated that a minister could discharge all his pastoral obligations in three days and that would leave him the rest of the week to pursue other interests. Many years later at a meeting of the

Synod of his church a man read from that pamphlet, pointing out the low view of ministry that it espoused. Then the man scornfully asked, "Did you write that?" Chalmers admitted that he had written it and explained: that in those days he aspired to be a professor of maths but added, "What is maths? It is magnitude and the proportion of magnitude, and in those days I had forgotten two magnitudes: the shortness of time and the length of eternity." We can covet a career that will ultimately deprive us of a more meaningful life. Let us have heavenly ambitions and covet the treasures of heaven.

If we are going to live for what this life has to offer then death spoils everything. If we are to avoid despair over a misspent life we need to have the perspective of the apostle Paul, who, while in prison and facing the possibility of death, wrote to his friends at Philippi, 'For me to live is Christ and to die is gain' (Philippians 1:21). How do we want to finish our days, like Solomon or like Paul? Jim Eliot, a martyred missionary, once said, "Only one life 'twill soon by past. Only what's done for Christ will last". If we covet the things of this world we cannot have a heavenly perspective. It would be sad indeed if we find ourselves on our deathbed wishing we had our time over again. It's not too late for us to realign our values with God's principles.

Advertising generates greed and unrealistic desires and expectations. People feel that they must have a certain object, model of car or make of kitchen. They feel that their home must look like the Ideal Homes Exhibition show-house or something that could be featured in *Homes & Gardens*[1] People feel they must go on foreign

---

[1] A U.K magazine established for over 80 years. Its blurb says that it, 'celebrates the beauty of classic and contemporary style. Real-life homes with stunning photography deliver inspirational decorating while remaining real and relevant. *Homes & Gardens* is the ultimate sourcebook of beautiful ideas and detailed information, inspiring its readers to become their own interior designers.'

holidays because their neighbours or friends are going. Advertising works on the basis of covetousness. That is the underlying principle. Many people feel that they must have brand name footwear and designer clothes. The internationally popular T.V. quiz show: *'Who wants to be a millionaire?'* and the national lottery appeal to the desire to satisfy every material whim. Many people say, "If only I won! Imagine the lifestyle I could have!"

It is easy to be discontented in this world. We imagine if only this or that our lives would be great. But people who believe that are deluding themselves. The underlying attitude is, if I had that I would be happy. John D. Rockefeller, (1839–1937) the U.S. industrialist, who founded the oil-refining company, Standard Oil (1870) was a multi-billionaire. When he was asked how much would make a person happy he answered, "Just a little bit more". Solomon wrote:

> He who loves silver will not be satisfied with silver; nor he who loves abundance, with increase. This also *is* vanity. When goods increase, they increase who eat them; so what profit have the owners except to see *them* with their eyes? The sleep of a labouring man *is* sweet, whether he eats little or much; but the abundance of the rich will not permit him to sleep. There is a severe evil *which* I have seen under the sun: riches kept for their owner to his hurt. But those riches perish through misfortune; when he begets a son, *there is* nothing in his hand. As he came from his mother's womb, naked shall he return, to go as he came; and he shall take nothing from his labour which he may carry away in his hand. (Ecclesiastes 5:10-15).

Violations of this commandment lead to violence, strife and discord among families and friends. Much history was determined by covetous attitudes. Luke 12 records the story of a man who spoke to Jesus concerning his inheritance from his father's death. He felt he hadn't got his fair share of the estate and asked Jesus to adjudicate on the matter. Jesus refused and instead told the parable about the Rich Fool which was getting at this man's attitude of heart. The point of that parable is that we should not be worldly but rather we should focus on eternity.

We must stop always looking over the fence. The lust for what other people have makes idols of things of no substance. In the New Testament Paul defines covetousness as idolatry, 'Therefore put to death your members which are on the earth: fornication, uncleanness, passion, evil desire, and covetousness, which is idolatry' (Colossians 3:5). Covetousness is a trial or difficulty that comes to us all but the believer should be able to cope with it. The writer to the Hebrews gives us some relevant advice, '*Let your* conduct *be* without covetousness; *be* content with such things as you have' (Hebrews 13:5). This is a vital principle for godly living. We must learn to be content. Paul's first letter to Timothy speaks on this topic and we would do well to take due notice of it in such a materialistic age:

> Now godliness with contentment is great gain. For we brought nothing into *this* world, *and it is* certain we can carry nothing out. And having food and clothing, with these we shall be content. But those who desire to be rich fall into temptation and a snare, and *into* many foolish and harmful lusts which drown men in destruction and perdition. For the love of money is a root of all *kinds of* evil, for which some have strayed from the faith in their greediness, and pierced themselves through with many sorrows. But you, O man of God, flee these things and pursue righteousness, godliness, faith, love, patience, gentleness (1 Timothy 6:6-11).

Rich or poor, we are all susceptible to covetousness, whatever our social standing or bank balance. Scripture warns us about this terrible disease of covetousness which has practical and wide ranging application.

There is an old Scandinavian fable that tells of a spider that came down from the lofty rafters of a barn on a single thread. He anchored that thread to a rafter beam and then used it as the main support of his world and weaved his way. He had chosen a very busy corner of the barn and waxed fat and prospered. One day in his prosperity he was walking across his web and he happened to notice this strand that reached up into the unseen distance. He had long since forgotten its significance and thought it was just a stray strand so he reached up and snapped it. Instantly his whole world caved in.

We sever the link with heaven at our peril. Our aspirations to prosper materially must not displace God from that foremost place in our hearts. We must be careful not to wax fat and forget the significance of that vital link with heaven. This commandment says:

> "You shall not covet your neighbour's house; you shall not covet your neighbour's wife, nor his male servant, nor his female servant, nor his ox, nor his donkey, nor anything that *is* your neighbour's"

Let us forsake covetousness and cultivate contentment. Let us rather covet a mansion in heaven. Let us, as the bride of Christ, covet the bridegroom. Let us say with the apostle Paul, 'I press toward the goal for the prize of the upward call of God in Christ Jesus' (Philippians 3:14).

Conclusion

E xodus 34 tells us that God proclaimed His name to Moses. In other words God revealed something essential about His nature. It is important, in the context of the commandments to understand the being and character of God. The following words give some insight into the character of God:

> "The LORD, the LORD God, merciful and gracious, longsuffering, and abounding in goodness and truth, keeping mercy for thousands, forgiving iniquity and transgression and sin, by no means clearing *the guilty*, visiting the iniquity of the fathers upon the children and the children's children to the third and the fourth generation" (Exodus 34:5-7).

The Almighty is both a just judge and a gracious God. To overemphasise or underemphasise either of these aspects of His character is to misrepresent Him. Chapter 32 of Exodus records that during Moses' absence from the camp at the foot of Mount Sinai there was great unrest amongst the people and they prevailed on Aaron to make a golden calf. These are the same people who had such an amazing demonstration of God's power. They had known His providential care and protection in such dramatic ways. It seems almost incredible, therefore, that they should turn so soon to idol worship. When Moses discovers what has happened he is angry and God too is angry with the people. But Moses intercedes and pleads with God on their behalf. In chapter 33 the word 'grace' is repeated many times. This is unexpected. Judgement is talked about but the overwhelming emphasis is on grace.

If we focus only on law then we are in a terrible and hopeless position. If we focus only on grace then we are in a position that is dangerous. Grace is related to the law. Jesus died because God takes His law seriously. The law was honoured by God. Jesus kept it on earth and died to pay the penalty of the broken law. We only understand grace when we take the law seriously and see what it cost God to provide all the benefits that flow from the grace of God in Christ.

When Moses came down from Mount Sinai the people were engaged in debauchery and idol worship. In his anger he smashed the tablets of stone. It is an incident which symbolises the fact that the law had been broken. So Moses went back to receive the law again. We might expect a simple restatement of the law but what we get first is God revealing his name. The names of God in both the Old Testament and the New Testament are very important because they reveal something of His character. The revelation to Moses showed God to be both holy and loving. He reveals that He is a gracious God. He takes the law seriously but He is concerned to convey to Moses that He is gracious. This is an interesting disclosure in a context where the people had sinned grievously. God was saying that the law is not all that there is to be known about Him. He declared that He was a God of grace.

What is God's grace? Grace is God's unmerited favour bestowed lavishly on His children. We, like the rebellious people of Israel at that time, deserve judgement and damnation. But God is gracious. This sovereign grace is His to give or withhold. If God sent everybody to hell He would not be doing anything wrong. He could have passed us by but He didn't. But this grace which is free to us cost God so much. He became poor that we might become rich. The grace that God bestows is not a minimal portion. It is not rationed. He didn't dispense it meanly. Rather God dispenses grace liberally, with largesse, from His magnanimous heart. The apostle Paul told the Romans that, 'where sin abounded, grace abounded much more' (Romans 5:20). There is nothing meagre about God's grace. The title of John Bunyan's biography, *Grace Abounding to the Chief of Sinners*, captures one man's appreciation of it. John Newton's hymn expresses his (and our) amazement at such astounding grace.

Amazing Grace

Amazing grace, how sweet the sound
That saved a wretch like me!
I once was lost, but now am found,
Was blind, but now I see.

'Twas grace that taught my heart to fear,
And grace my fears relieved;
How precious did that grace appear,
The hour I first believed!

Through many dangers, toils and snares,
I have already come;
'Tis grace has brought me safe thus far,
And grace will lead me home.

The Lord has promised good to me,
His word my hope secures;
He will my shield and portion be,
As long as life endures.

Yes, when this flesh and heart shall fail,
And mortal life shall cease;

> I shall possess, within the veil,
>
> A life of joy and peace.
>
> The earth shall soon dissolve like snow,
>
> The sun forbear to shine;
>
> But God, who called me here below,
>
> Will be forever mine.
>
> When I've been there ten thousand years,
>
> Bright shining as the sun,
>
> I've no less days to sing God's praise
>
> Than when I first begun.[1]

As disciples of Christ we are not called into His family because God saw some potential in us that He could work on and develop. We are not a cut above others. We are undeserving. In fact we are hell-deserving sinners. We begin with grace and we have to continue with grace. We tend to get muddled with this and try to go it alone or only occasionally fall back on grace. We also end with grace. Heaven awaits us not because of our virtuous lives but because of His atoning sacrifice. Thus we commence, continue and complete this spiritual life with grace. It is truly amazing. We ought to be amazed by it. We should never take it for granted. Our lives must display gratitude for that great grace. This is best seen in our devotion to God but it must also be evident in our relationships with each other. Thus Paul told the Ephesians, 'be kind to one another, tenderhearted, forgiving one another, even as God in Christ forgave you' (Ephesians 4:32).

God has not been miserly with grace. He did not merely give a certain quota of limited grace that can be exhausted. It is not rationed like butter and meat and other goods were rationed in Britain during World War II. Grace is not like that. We don't have to spread it thinly.

---

[1] John Newton, 1725-1807.

God was not tight-fisted, rather He was open-handed and we ought to show something of that likeness in our human relationships. God's grace is sufficient. It is always enough. It never runs short. He never gives us less than we need. He gives us just what is appropriate.

It has already been said that the commandments are not a stepladder to heaven. But neither are they a cudgel to beat us into submission. Rather they are given to draw us to the Saviour that we might cast ourselves utterly on Him. The Bible is written in two languages; Hebrew and Greek. But the story of the Bible is written in two words, LAW and GRACE. There are several mountains mentioned in Scripture but the two most significant mountains are Sinai and Calvary. On Sinai God is seen in glory and His sovereignty, power and holiness are emphasised. On, Calvary, the mount of crucifixion, God's grace is manifested in an unparalleled way. But grace is evident on Sinai and holiness is evident on Calvary. These two hills show the two aspects of God's character.

The commandments compel us to see our failure under the law. This failure in turn drives us to Christ in faith. Christ alone kept the law. Christ alone fulfilled the law's requirements for an atoning sacrifice. Let us cherish Christ in our hearts and commend Him to those still under the curse of the law.